Feasting Galore
Irish-Style

Hippocrene is NUMBER ONE in
International Cookbooks

Africa and Oceania
Best of Regional African Cooking
Egyptian Cooking
Good Food from Australia
Traditional South African Cookery
Taste of Eritrea

Asia and Near East
The Best of Taiwanese Cuisine
Imperial Mongolian Cooking
The Joy of Chinese Cooking
Healthy South Indian Cooking
The Indian Spice Kitchen
Best of Goan Cooking
Best of Kashmiri Cooking
Afghan Food & Cookery
The Art of Persian Cooking
The Art of Turkish Cooking
The Art of Uzbek Cooking

Mediterranean
Best of Greek Cuisine
Taste of Malta
A Spanish Family Cookbook
Tastes of North Africa

Western Europe
Art of Dutch Cooking
Best of Austrian Cuisine
A Belgian Cookbook
Cooking in the French Fashion (bilingual)
Celtic Cookbook
Cuisines of Portuguese Encounters
English Royal Cookbook
The Swiss Cookbook
Traditional Recipes from Old England
The Art of Irish Cooking
Feasting Galore Irish-Style
Traditional Food from Scotland
Traditional Food from Wales
The Scottish-Irish Pub and Hearth
  Cookbook
A Treasury of Italian Cuisine (bilingual)

Scandinavia
Best of Scandinavian Cooking
The Best of Finnish Cooking
The Best of Smorgasbord Cooking
Good Food from Sweden

Central Europe
All Along the Danube
All Along the Rhine
Best of Albanian Cooking
Best of Croatian Cooking
Bavarian Cooking
Traditional Bulgarian Cooking
The Best of Czech Cooking
The Best of Slovak Cooking
The Art of Hungarian Cooking
Hungarian Cookbook
Art of Lithuanian Cooking
Polish Heritage Cookery
The Best of Polish Cooking
Old Warsaw Cookbook
Old Polish Traditions
Treasury of Polish Cuisine (bilingual)
Poland's Gourmet Cuisine
Taste of Romania
Taste of Latvia

Eastern Europe
The Best of Russian Cooking
Traditional Russian Cuisine (bilingual)
The Best of Ukrainian Cuisine

Americas
Argentina Cooks
Cooking the Caribbean Way
Mayan Cooking
The Honey Cookbook
The Art of Brazilian Cookery
The Art of South American Cookery
Old Havana Cookbook (bilingual)

Feasting Galore
Irish-Style

Recipes and Food Lore from the Emerald Isle

Maura Laverty

Foreword by the Rt. Hon. Robert Briscoe
Former Lord Mayor of Dublin

Hippocrene Books
New York

Hippocrene Books Inc. edition, 2001

Copyright 1952, 1955 by Maura Laverty
Copyright© 1957, 1961 by Maura Laverty

Originally published as *Feasting Galore: Recipes and Food Lore from Ireland* by Holt, Rinehart and Winston, New York

ISBN 0-7818-0869-3

For information, address:
HIPPOCRENE BOOKS, INC.
171 Madison Avenue
New York, NY 10016

For our daughter, Maeve, who has always been
queen of our kitchen and heart of our home

Foreword

I have always wished that Maura Laverty were as well known in the United States as she is at home. Her writings would help to kill that fictitious character, "the stage Irishman." Here she is a leading playwright and novelist, and her articles and broadcasts on good cooking have made her name a household word throughout the length and breadth of the country. The qualities with which she has achieved distinction as a writer are her dignity, sincerity, and true understanding of the Irish character—qualities which are always leavened by her keen sense of humor.

While theater audiences and readers wish that she would devote herself entirely to the writing of plays and novels, Irish housewives are grateful for her incursions into the kitchen. For Maura Laverty is not merely an authority on modern cooking. Her knowledge of Irish traditional cooking makes her a leader in this field, and this knowledge she has gained from a detailed study of the lives of the early Irish saints which are our chief source of information concerning the domestic ways of the ancient Irish.

I believe that *Feasting Galore* will carry the nostalgic and appetizing aroma of the Irish kitchen to our exiles all over the world. It is my hope that to readers who cannot claim that "drop of Irish blood" it may prove that home life in Ireland retains a dignity and graciousness, and that the cooking of our country is not limited—as so many seem to believe—to Irish stew and stirabout.

Robert Briscoe

LL.D., T.D., T.C., P.C.

Contents

4 Soups, 48

5 Fish, 57

6 *Vegetables,* 69

Salads, 78

7 *Meat, Poultry, Game,* 80

8 Fast-Day Feasts, 96

Eggs, Cheese, Cereals, 96

9 Sauces, Sweet and Savory, 103

Savory Sauces, 106

10 Jellies, Jams, Pickles, 112

Feasting Galore

Ballad of an Irish Wheat Field

Walk softly, O man, past an acre of wheat,
  With awe in your heart and your face.
Walk humbly, O man, and with reverent feet,
For strength slumbers here—Can't you feel its heart beat?
And beauty's own couch is an acre of wheat,
  And holiness dwells in this place.

Breathe gently, O breeze, on the grain-heavy ears,
  That drank long and deep of spring rain.
O breeze, ripple gently the yellow-tipped spears.
Our little ones, caught in the rush of the years,
Need growth that is stored in the wheat's golden ears
  All mother-ripe now with smooth grain.

Sing sweetly, O birds, as you skim the rich field,
  And sprinkle your hyssop of song,
For here in each silken-caped kernel is sealed
The secret of living. The liberal yield
Will strengthen and quicken, O birds of the field,
  And comfort the earth's hungry throng.

Shine kindly, O sun, keep it warmly alive.
    On this field lay a tender caress,
For here is the reason men struggle and strive
And strain, sweat and anguish and battle and drive.
And life's spent for wheat just to keep men alive.
    O sun, let your rays kindly bless.

Walk softly, O man, past an acre of wheat,
    O birds, mute your silver-splashed mirth!
O breeze, hold your breathing! O sun, shed your heat!
For here is the food that God gave us to eat. . . .
The Body of Christ comes from sanctified wheat,
    Twice-blessed be this fruit of the earth!

1

Bread

"Give us this day our daily bread . . ."
Sermon on the Mount

"I believe in bread-making" is the first and most important article of my culinary *Credo*. I applaud every effort to revive this kindliest of domestic arts. My enthusiasm is not based merely on dietary arguments, but on my belief in the traditional goodness of bread. I believe that the woman who bakes her family's bread brings this goodness into the kitchen. Irish tinkers often lay a crust of bread on the breast of a corpse. This is not to say that they intend the bread as food for the next world, but that they look on bread as a holy substance. "The dear God's bread," they call it. Their habit of carrying a crust in their pocket as a protection against evil spirits dates from Elizabethan times. There is a couplet by Herrick which goes:

> In your pocket for a trust,
> Carry nothing but a crust,
>   For that holy piece of bread
>   Charms the danger and the dread.

And plain bread *can* charm—as Mrs. Donnelly discovered to her chagrin that time Brian Feeney was courting the domestic economy instructress who is now his happy wife.

Brian's mother was more sincere than is usual with widowed mothers of only sons when she said she would be glad to see Brian bring in a wife. "I'm poor company for him," she often said. "And in a big old place like this there's more work than can be managed by an elderly woman like myself with only a raw servant girl to give her a hand."

That was why she was genuinely pleased when Brian, at thirty-five, suddenly showed all the signs and symptoms of a man who is courting. Mrs. Feeney passed no remark when he took to shaving himself every evening after the cows were milked and the supper was over. She never once asked him where he was going when, changed from his working clothes into his Sunday suit, he set off on his bicycle down the Newbridge road. In her heart she may have said, "Heaven grant she's a nice girl who'll make him happy," or, "May she bring peace and content into this house, whoever she is." But though she felt a natural curiosity, she had little anxiety. She knew that she could trust her son, and that he would tell her all she ought to know whenever the time would be ripe.

Mrs. Donnelly anticipated him with the news.

There were few in Ballyderrig who welcomed the coming of Mrs. Donnelly. "The Raven," she was called. She well deserved her nickname. Never did a bird of ill omen take more delight in carrying news that was calculated to disturb and alarm.

That Sunday afternoon when she called on Mrs. Feeney, she came with a pound of black-currant jam and a stone of sympathy. Carefully she lowered her bulk onto a chair which, under her overflowing width, took on the aspect of doll's house furniture. She sighed gustily. The chair creaked loudly. "Do you know what it is, Mary?" she opened. "The longer I live, the more I realize that I'm as well off to be childless."

"Why do you say that, Sarah?" Mrs. Feeney asked with kindness.

"For the simple reason that I'm able to enjoy my old age in comfort without being upset by the carryings-on of young people." Mrs. Donnelly's broad face was wreathed in complacency. "My heart goes out to every unfortunate woman with a marriageable son."

"Ah, I don't know, now," Mrs. Feeney said reasonably. "Take my Brian. He never gave me an hour's worry in his life."

This was the opening for which Mrs. Donnelly had been maneuvering. She leaned forward, a podgy hand planted on either knee. "Heaven help you, Mary," she sympathized. "It's little you know how he's planning to bring a strange woman in on top of you."

"Oh, *that*?" There was relief in Mrs. Feeney's voice. For a second or two, Sarah Donnelly had had her worried. "For Brian to take a wife would be no upset to me, Sarah. I'm more than pleased that he's showing signs of being interested in some girl in Newbridge."

Mrs. Donnelly was annoyed. So this was the way Mary Feeney was going to take it? So she was going to make out that she didn't care?

Mrs. Feeney smiled her gentle smile. "I'll be happy to welcome Brian's wife. I know that he'll bring no woman in here except one that's suitable."

Mrs. Donnelly shook her head in sad commiseration. "Heaven give you sense, you creature," she said. "Brian is going to shame and humiliate you." Satisfaction gushed in her as she saw alarm leap at last into Mary Feeney's eyes and heard the other woman's urgent, "Who is she? Who or what is she, Sarah?"

"A domestic economy instructress—that's what she is!" Mrs. Donnelly sat back. "She's a highfalutin lassie with strings of letters after her name. A college-trained cook with classy notions about dressed-up dishes, who'll come in here and make little of your cooking and who'll make your son wonder how he ever managed to reach manhood on the food you fed him. Heaven comfort you, Mary Feeney, because it's comfort you'll be needing."

There was little that Mrs. Feeney could say. Put as Sarah Donnelly had put it, the situation offered poor prospect of her being able to go to her grave in peace and contentment. She realized now that her happy acceptance of Brian's courtship had been based on visions of herself imparting all she knew of homemaking to a girl who would look up to her and respect her and treat her as an oracle. The thought of having to make way for a scornful college-trained cook filled her with woe.

She was plunged into deeper woe when Brian came to her a few days later to tell her the news he thought she would be delighted to hear. "You'll love Anna, mother," he said. "She's a grand girl—a girl after your own heart. I'd like to bring her to tea next Sunday."

When Mrs. Donnelly called that evening she found Mary Feeney sitting, depressed and worried, with a cookery book in her hand. "It's what to give her for her tea that has me distracted," she confessed, patting her soft gray hair in an agitated way. "If it was dinner now. But I'm the worst hand in the world when it comes to making fancy cakes."

It was true. As was the case with most of the farming women of Ballyderrig, the making of fancy cakes was as foreign to Mrs. Feeney as going upstairs to bed is foreign to a tinker. Plain bread was a different story. When it came to making plain soda bread there was no one in the County Kildare who could hold a candle to her. The dough of her bread was as light and as white as bog cotton. The crust was always brittle and richly brown, with never a crack or a seam. The shape had a symmetry usually to be seen only in advertisements, and the flavor was the true sweet nutty flavor of perfectly baked wheat.

But while good soda bread was all right in its way, it would not suffice of itself to make an attractive tea table, particularly when the guest of honor was a girl on whom Mrs. Feeney had to make a good impression. More particularly still when that girl was a domestic-economy teacher who had learned all there is to be known about the grandeur of stylish confectionery.

"You're in a sad fix, to be sure," Mrs. Donnelly sympathized. "Isn't it the pity of the world that you never mastered the making of sweet cakes? A nice sponge cake, like mine, or a nice marble cake like the one I make with four eggs—that's the kind of cake to make an elegant tea table that wouldn't bring shame on a woman before her future daughter-in-law, even if she were to have all the letters of the alphabet after her name."

"What will I do, at all?" Mrs. Feeney lamented.

"And isn't it a most unfortunate thing," Mrs. Donnelly pursued relentlessly, "to be living in a backward place like this where a nice fancy cake is not to be bought? You could, of course, send in to New-bridge or Kildare for one. But how would you be sure that it wouldn't be stale? Or that what went into it wasn't of the cheapest quality? A trained instructress would be the first to notice a thing like that."

Mrs. Feeney threw herself on The Raven's mercy. She pleaded. "Sarah, would you ever make a couple of cakes for me? A couple of real nice ones? I'll give you all the butter and eggs and sugar you want."

"With pleasure," Mrs. Donnelly said, and she meant it. She would enjoy telling Ballyderrig how Mary Feeney had had to call on her for help.

"You'll come to tea yourself on Sunday?" Mrs. Feeney invited, since there was no way out of it.

"With pleasure," Sarah Donnelly repeated. To be able to give a firsthand account of the new Mrs. Feeney would be better still.

If appearance and manner were all that counted, Mrs. Feeney would have said that Anna Shiels was the daughter-in-law for whom she had been praying. She was a slim, brown-haired girl with good gray eyes and with a sweet and merry gentleness. It gave the elderly woman great happiness to see the way she looked at Brian and he at her.

The table looked nice. Mrs. Donnelly had made a sponge cake with a swirl of white icing to crown it, and her famous marble cake had risen nicely. For those who might like a bit of something plain to start there was a plate of Mrs. Feeney's soda bread, thinly cut and well buttered.

Anna Shiels was one of those who like to start their tea with plain bread. She took a slice, and then another slice, and another slice after that.

"Here, have a bit of sweet cake," Mrs. Donnelly urged. "What about a scrap of sponge? Or a nice slice of marble cake?"

"I'd rather have this delicious soda bread, thanks," Anna said, helping herself to yet another slice. "I never tasted the like of it in my life. It would win a prize anywhere. How on earth do you make it, Mrs. Feeney?"

Pride and happiness dawned like the rising sun in Mrs. Feeney's face. "It's simple," she explained eagerly. "Just take the full of the little blue jug of milk, as much as you think of flour, a taste of salt and a suspicion of bread soda. And then you mix it—but you don't wet it, if you know what I mean."

Anna said seriously, "I always think it's in the cooking of plain food that a real cook proves herself. Take sweet cakes, now. Any child could make a sweet cake that will pass. It stands to reason that if you mix up a lot of nice-tasting things like eggs and butter and sugar you'll be bound to have something that will turn out well, particularly if you put a slather of icing over it. But there's no way of disguising badly made soda bread. Yours is a real treat, Mrs. Feeney. Would you think me very greedy if I had another slice?"

"Eat away, alanna," Mrs. Feeney said, her heart dancing to this sweet music.

"You know," Anna confided, "it's only after leaving college that a girl like myself finds out all she has to learn. Anyone at all can cook in a city kitchen where there's nothing to be done but look after the cooker. But the cook who really deserves admiration is the woman who can turn out good food in a farmhouse kitchen in between churning and feeding calves and fowl. How does she ever manage to get around it all?"

"No difficulty at all, Anna," Mrs. Feeney assured her, and her eyes were shining. "No difficulty in the world, child. All a young married woman needs is to have someone experienced at hand to give her advice now and again and to show her the way."

When the tea was over and Brian stood up to go out to the milking, Mrs. Donnelly decided that it was time for her to leave. "Good evening to you all," she said shortly as she left.

Mrs. Feeney and Anna did not miss her company. They had a very enjoyable time looking through photographs of Brian as a baby.

Soda bread, as all the world knows, is the traditional bread of Ireland. Unpatriotic though it may seem, pride of place in any modern cookbook must be given to yeast bread—for the very good reason that yeast bread is better for us. When we add bicarbonate of soda to foods, we reduce their content of Vitamin B1—the all-important vitamin necessary for muscular energy, steady nerves, healthy skin, good appetite, sound digestion. (Because it is especially important to expectant and nursing mothers it is known as "the women's vitamin.") Yeast is especially rich in Vitamin B1. It is present in flour and in milk—which is why when we make bread with yeast, we make three good things trebly valuable.

Yeast bread is easy to make.

Basic Recipe for Yeast Bread

Ingredients: 12 cups sifted all-purpose flour, 2 packages active dry yeast, 2¾ cups tepid milk and water (half and half), 2-4 tablespoons butter, 2 tablespoons salt, 1 tablespoon sugar.

Method: Melt the butter in the milk and water. Mix the yeast with the sugar. Add to it about 1 cup of the milk mixture. Sift the flour with the salt, make a well in the center and pour in the yeast. Sprinkle flour on top, cover and leave in a warm place until the yeast forms a honeycomb. Mix to a dough with the remainder of the milk, turn onto a floured board, and knead well for at least 15 minutes. There is more to this kneading than meets the eye. The fineness of the texture of yeast bread depends on proper and thorough kneading. Push the dough from you with the heel of your fist and pull in toward you with your fingers. Turn it clockwise as you knead. It is a one-two-three movement and to do it properly you must get rhythm into it. When you have the bread kneaded put it back into the bowl, brush it with butter, cover, and leave it in a warm place until it has doubled its bulk. Knead it again, divide it into two loaves, put them in greased pans, brush with butter, cover, and leave them in a warm place until they have doubled their bulk. Into a hot (450°) oven with them now to bake for 1 hour. To make sure they're done, tap the bottom. If the sound is hollow, the bread is done. Stand them on their sides while cooling; wrap them in tea towels if you want a soft crust.

Yeast Bread (Overnight Method)

The overnight or cold-rising method of yeast breadmaking halves the work. The dough will rise while you sleep. Next morning, turn it out on a floured board, knead lightly for a couple of minutes. Shape in loaves, place in greased tins, cover, and allow to rise about 15 minutes. Bake as usual.

>   N.B.: Prepare dough as for basic recipe but use *cold* milk or milk-and-water (half and half). Leave overnight to rise in a greased covered container (a bread bin or plastic bag). Brush the top of the dough with butter to prevent the formation of a skin which would check the rising of the dough.

Whole-Meal Bread (Yeast)

(By whole meal, sometimes called whole-wheat flour or wheaten meal, is meant ground wheat composed of 100-per-cent wheat kernel. Although it is possible to make excellent bread of whole meal alone, most cooks like to add a small portion of white flour to ensure better cutting consistency.)

Ingredients: 8 cups whole meal, 4 cups tepid milk-and-water (half and half), 3 tablespoons salt, 3 tablespoons sugar, 2 packages dry yeast.

Method: Warm the whole meal and mix with the salt in a large warm bowl. Mix the yeast with the sugar and add to it ½ cup of the milk-and-water mixture (the liquid should be lukewarm). Make a well in the center of the whole meal, pour in the yeast mixture. Sprinkle a little of the whole meal on top and leave in a warm place until the yeast froths. Stir with a wooden spoon until the meal is evenly wetted (the dough should be wetter than when making whole-meal bread with baking soda, p. 17). Grease 3 large loaf tins and warm them well. Spoon the dough (which should not be kneaded) into the tins. Cover with cloth and leave in a warm place until it increases its original bulk by half. Then bake for 50 minutes to 1 hour in a 450° oven. When baked, turn the loaves upside down on a wire rack and leave until cold. If the loaves do not come out of the tin easily, leave them for a few minutes. Whole-meal bread is best kept for twenty-four hours before cutting.

FANCY YEAST BREADS AND BUNS

Barmbrack

(The term "barbrack" for an Irish fruit loaf or cake does not derive from barm or leaven. It is a corruption of the Irish word *arán breac* which means "speckled bread.")

Halloween in Ireland would be unthinkable without barmbrack, the sweet and sticky-crusted loaf which foretells one's fortune for the coming year. Into the fruity dough we knead (paper-wrapped to guard against choking or appendicitis) a ring for marriage, a silver coin for wealth, and a button for single blessedness.

For 2 large barmbracks you will need—

Ingredients: 7½ cups sifted all-purpose flour, 2 packages dry yeast, 1½ tablespoons salt, 3 cups warm milk-and-water (half and half), 1 cup sugar, 6 tablespoons butter, 2½ cups raisins, ¾ cup currants, 2 teaspoons allspice, ¾ cup chopped citrus peel.

Method: Sift flour, allspice, and salt into a large bowl. Mix the yeast with 1 teaspoon of the sugar and add half of the warm milk-and-water. Make a well in center of flour, pour in the yeast mixture, sprinkle a little flour on top and leave about 20 minutes until the yeast honeycombs. Mix in the flour, add remaining liquid, and mix thoroughly. Knead to a ball and turn out on a floured board. Knead until the dough no longer feels sticky and comes away clean from the board. Wash and grease the bowl, return the dough to it, cover and leave until it doubles its bulk. If left in a warm place (an oven warming compartment) this will take about 30 minutes; left on the kitchen table, about 3 hours. Turn the dough onto a floured board, flatten to a large round, place butter, sugar, fruit, and peel in the middle, and work in these ingredients by squeezing and kneading until they are evenly incorporated in the dough. At this point, work in the paper-wrapped charms. Return the dough again to the greased bowl, cover, and leave to rise for 30 minutes. Divide the dough in two and shape to fit two 2-lb baking tins. Half fill the tins, cover, and leave in a warm place to rise to the top of tins. Bake about 50 minutes in a hot (475°) oven, reducing the heat to 450° for the last 15 minutes of baking. Five minutes before the barmbracks are done, brush with sugar and water in equal quantities.

Currant Buns

Ingredients: 6 cups sifted flour, ½ cup raisins, ½ cup currants, ⅓ cup candied peel, 8 tablespoons (¼ pound) butter, 1 cup sugar, 2 teaspoons salt, 1 cup lukewarm milk, 1 package dry yeast.

Method: Mix yeast with ⅔ cup sugar. Sift flour with salt. Melt butter in lukewarm milk. Add yeast and milk mixture to flour and beat well. Cover and leave in a warm place until mixture doubles its bulk. Turn onto floured board, spread with fruit and part of remaining sugar, and knead well. Cover and leave to rise 30 minutes. Shape into buns (these quantities will make about 20). Place on greased baking tin, leave in a warm place 20 minutes, then bake 15 minutes at 500°. Just before they are done, brush with water or egg white and sprinkle with remaining sugar.

Fairy Rings

These delicacies are very much more palatable than the oaten cakes dipped in honey which were the dessert of our ancestors. The Irish Mist is a liqueur made from old Irish whiskey, herbal essences, and honey. It is the only Irish liqueur, and is today's nearest approach to the heather wine or mead which was so prized long ago and was known as "the dainty drink of nobles."

6 savarin dough rings (baba)   1 package green gelatine (prepared according to directions on package)
1 cup heavy cream
½ cup Irish Mist liqueur

Dip baked rings in the liqueur. Fill each ring with whipped cream and sprinkle with the chopped green gelatine.

Hot Cross Buns

As Lent draws to a close, Good Friday hot cross buns are a welcome break in the Lenten fast.

Ingredients: 6 cups sifted flour, 3 eggs, 1 teaspoon each cinnamon and ginger, 8 tablespoons butter, 1 package dry yeast, 1 cup raisins, ½ cup currants, ¾ cup candied citrus peel, 2 teaspoons salt, ¼ cup granulated sugar, ¾ cup sifted confectioner's sugar (about), 1 cup milk.

Method: Mix yeast with 2 teaspoons granulated sugar. Heat milk to lukewarm and mix with 2 of the eggs, well beaten. Add melted butter to milk and combine with yeast. Sift flour with salt and spices. Add remaining granulated sugar. Make a well in center and pour in milk mixture. Sprinkle a little flour on top and leave in a warm place until the yeast begins to work. Work the flour into the liquid with hands so as to make a soft dough. Turn out on a floured board and knead 5 to 10 minutes. Shape into a ball, place in a lightly greased bowl, cover with a cloth, and leave in a warm place until the dough doubles in bulk. Turn the dough onto a floured board and work into it the fruit and peel. Shape the dough into 24 buns. Flatten and place on a greased baking sheet about one inch apart. Separate the remaining egg. Brush the buns with the beaten yolk mixed with a little milk and leave to rise in a warm place until double in bulk. Make a deep cross in each bun. Bake 20 minutes in a 400° oven. Mix the egg white with the confectioner's sugar and glaze the buns with this mixture while they are still warm.

Sally Lunn

The English like to claim this feather-light teacake as their own. But we Irish have just as much right to it. Didn't Sarah Curran, the beloved of bold Robert Emmet, bake Sally Lunns for her father's famous Sunday-night parties? Here, under the cover of teacup clatter and intellectual talk, Sarah's love affair with the doomed young rebel blossomed unknown to her father, who, still smarting because his wife had run away with a clergyman, would have liked to have kept his daughter in purdah.

Ingredients: 3 cups sifted flour, 1 teaspoon salt, ½ package dry yeast,

2 teaspoons sugar, 2 tablespoons butter, 1 egg, a little less than 1 cup milk, 2 tablespoons sugar for glaze.

Method: Sift flour with salt. Make a well in it. Mix yeast with 2 teaspoons sugar, add melted butter, beaten egg, and lukewarm milk (reserve 1 tablespoon milk for glaze). Pour yeast mixture into flour, mix to a dough, and knead for a few minutes on a floured board. Grease well 2 small cake tins, divide dough between them, cover with a cloth, and leave in a warm place until dough has risen to tops of tins. Bake 15 minutes at 450°, or until well browned. Brush with milk, sprinkle with sugar, and return to oven 5 minutes.

Sunday Tea Cakes

Ingredients: 4 cups sifted flour, 2 teaspoons salt, 1 package dry yeast, 2 teaspoons sugar, 4 tablespoons lard, ½ cup boiling water, ½ cup milk, ½ cup currants, ⅓ cup candied peel, 1 cup white seedless raisins, milk and sugar for glaze.

Method: Sift flour with salt. Mix yeast with 2 teaspoons sugar, add ½ cup lukewarm milk. Make a well in center of flour, pour in yeast mixture, sprinkle a little flour on top, and leave to honeycomb in a warm place about 20 minutes. Dissolve lard in boiling water, add milk mixture. Leave until lukewarm. Add this mixture to flour and mix to a smooth dough. Turn onto floured board, sprinkle with fruit, and knead well. Divide the dough into 6 balls, flatten, and pierce with fork. Place on greased and floured baking sheet, cover, and leave to rise 30 minutes in warm place. Bake 20 minutes in hot (450°) oven. Five minutes before the cakes are done, brush with milk and sprinkle with sugar.

SODA BREADS

N.B.: Sour milk or milk from the Buttermilk Plant—p. 20—or Winter Buttermilk—p. 20—may be used instead of buttermilk in any Soda Bread recipe.

Basic Recipe for Soda Bread

Ingredients: 4 cups sifted flour, 2 teaspoons salt, 2 teaspoons sugar, 2 teaspoons baking soda, buttermilk to mix (about 1 cup).

Method: Sift dry ingredients together several times. Make a well in center. Pour in buttermilk gradually, mixing in the flour from the sides. (The mixture should not be too dry.) Turn it out on a floured board, knead lightly for a few minutes, pat the dough to a round and cut a cross on it to keep it from cracking in the baking. (Let the cuts go over the sides of the cake to make sure of this.) Brush with milk and bake at once in a hot (450°) oven for 45 minutes. If you have any doubts about "doneness," tap the bottom of the pan. If it sounds hollow it is done. (When using milk from the buttermilk plant, it doesn't hurt the bread to let it stand 15 minutes before baking.)

Some people like to add ½ teaspoon of cream of tartar or 1 teaspoon baking powder. I think this is unnecessary. The baking soda and good buttermilk provide all the leaven needed.

Griddle Bread

Roll out Soda Bread dough 1-inch thick. Cut it in four farls (scones) or triangles. Cook them on a hot, floured griddle, 10 minutes on each side.

Treacle (Molasses) Bread

Increase the sugar in basic Soda Bread recipe to 2 tablespoons and add to the milk ½ cup of treacle (molasses). A beaten egg may be added as well, and 4 tablespoons of butter rubbed into the flour. Raisins, currants, and chopped nuts make this a party cake. Cook as for Soda Bread.

Seedy Bread

Use recipe for Soda Bread. Increase the sugar to 2 tablespoons. Rub 4 tablespoons of lard into the flour and add 1 tablespoon of caraway seeds.

Whole-Meal Bread (1)

Ingredients: 4½ cups whole meal, 1 cup sifted flour, 2 teaspoons salt, 2 teaspoons baking soda, 1 teaspoon cream of tartar. For liquid, use buttermilk, sour milk, or milk from the buttermilk plant (approximately 1½ cups).

Method: Sift together the flour, soda, salt, and cream of tartar. Mix well with the whole meal. Make a well in center and gradually mix in

sufficient liquid to make a stiff dough. Turn onto a floured board and
knead lightly until free from cracks. Form into a round cake and cut a
cross on the top to keep the cake from cracking in the baking. Bake at once
in a 450° oven for 1 hour.

Whole-Meal Bread (2)

Ingredients: 2¾ cups whole meal, 1 cup sifted white flour, 1 tablespoon
sugar, 1 tablespoon bacon dripping, 2 teaspoons salt, 2 teaspoons baking
soda, buttermilk to mix.

Method: Sift the salt and baking soda with the flour. Mix the sugar with
the whole meal. Add the flour and mix well. Rub in the bacon dripping.
Make a well in center and gradually mix in sufficient buttermilk to make
a stiff dough. Turn onto a floured board, knead lightly, turn upside down
and form into a round cake. Make a cross on top of the cake and bake on
a floured tin for 45 minutes in a 450° oven.

Whole-Meal Bread (3)

Ingredients: 2¾ cups whole meal, 1 cup sifted white flour, 2 teaspoons
each baking soda and cream of tartar, ¾ teaspoon salt, 1 tablespoon
sugar, buttermilk to mix (about ¾ cup).

Method: Sift the salt, sugar, cream of tartar, and baking soda with the
white flour. Mix thoroughly with the wheaten meal. Add sufficient buttermilk to make a stiff dough. (Too much liquid makes heavy bread.) Press
the dough lightly into a greased loaf tin and bake about 45 minutes in a
450° oven.

Oaten Bread

There was little bread eaten by the poor of Ireland in ancient
times. Their staple fare was stirabout made with oatmeal—exactly
like today's breakfast porridge. The nourishing effects of Irish stirabout seem to have been recognized even on the Continent. We find
St. Jerome demolishing an adversary from Munster with the scathing
comment, "a great fool of a fellow, swelled out with Irish stirabout."

For bread, oatmeal was most generally used. Bread was made in
loaves of two sizes. The larger was called a "man-baking" and the

smaller a "woman-baking." The bread was leavened with yeast, or with barm made by fermenting flour with water (the "winter butter-milk" of many parts of Ireland today). Or it was leavened with a piece of sour dough kept back from the previous baking. This custom still prevails in parts of Westmeath where the piece of sour dough is called "blessed bread."

Oaten Health Bread

Ingredients: 4 cups each flour, whole meal, and flake oatmeal; 1 table-spoon sugar, 4 tablespoons butter, 2 packages dry yeast, 1 tablespoon salt, 2 cups milk, 1 cup boiling water.

Method: Sift together flour, whole meal, flake oatmeal, and salt. Mix the yeast with the sugar. Dissolve the butter in the boiling water and add to the milk. Add a cupful of the tepid milk-and-water to the yeast-sugar mixture. Make a well in the center of the flour and pour in the yeast. Sprinkle a little flour on top and set in a warm place until the yeast honey-combs. Add the remainder of the tepid milk-and-water, mix well, turn out onto a floured board, and knead well for at least 10 minutes. Return to the bowl, cover with a cloth, and leave in a warm place until the dough doubles its bulk. Cook 50 minutes in a hot (475°) oven.

Once upon a time there was an Irish tinker whose virility and longevity were the pride and wonder of his tribe. Generations came and went, and still the old gentleman flourished like a green bay tree. Legends were built around the man who never sickened, never grew old. And when the caravans halted at night, the smoke of the camp-fires was thick with stories of the mysterious and jealously guarded elixir with which the patriarch preserved his strength and youthful-ness.

But even the strongest elixirs are not proof against spear thrusts. On the eve of the day when the sturdy old Casanova was about to take unto himself his twenty-second bride, he was found spitted to a beech tree—dispatched (many suspected) by a jealous swain 125 years his junior. A search of his caravan revealed the elixir. It was fermented milk.

Since then, science has confirmed that the fermented "milks" such as winter buttermilk and milk from the buttermilk plant (see recipes below) are undeniable sources of health and long life. Their value lies in the "friendly" bacteria which these milks contain.

Buttermilk Plant

Mix 2 tablespoons sugar with 1 package dry yeast. Gradually add 1 pint milk mixed with 1 pint water (the mixture should be tepid). Cover and leave for 2 days at room temperature, or until the "milk" smells and tastes like buttermilk. When you want to use the milk for drinking or baking, strain it through a colander lined with fine muslin. Then gently pour over residue in colander a cup of tepid water, to rinse off all sour milk. To start a new lot of "buttermilk," scrape the "plant" from the muslin, place it in a scalded vessel, and add 1 quart tepid milk-and-water (half and half). Cover and leave as before in a warm place to increase and multiply.

That first ounce of yeast will go on growing, producing buttermilk until the end of time. But the plant must be given a certain amount of care.

1. It must be strained at least every 5 days.
2. Make sure that the milk-and-water mixture is never more than tepid. Strong heat kills yeast.
3. Cleanliness is very important. The careful rinsing after straining and the scalding of the container are necessary if the plant is to live.

Winter Buttermilk

This is an excellent substitute for buttermilk when the cows go dry. Use exactly as buttermilk.

¼ cup flake oatmeal	2 medium raw potatoes, grated
2 medium potatoes, cooked and mashed	6 cups water

Mix flake oatmeal to a paste with 1 cup of water. Put this in a large jug or crock. Add the potatoes and remaining water. Cover and leave in a warm place for two days, stirring occasionally. When baking, pour off carefully as much liquid as is needed, without disturbing the sediment. Add fresh water to make up the amount used. Stir, cover, and again leave in a warm place until the next baking. Every two weeks, make a fresh supply.

FANCY LOAVES

Use a well-greased loaf pan. Having baked the loaf for the time specified in recipe, test for doneness (since ovens vary). To test: insert skewer in center; if it comes out clean, loaf is cooked. Most fancy loaves have a crack on top crust—this is characteristic and is not a fault. Do not cut for 24 hours after baking.

Convent Loaf

Ingredients: 4 cups sifted flour, 1 cup (½ pound) butter, ¾ cup sugar, 3 teaspoons baking powder, 2 teaspoons caraway seeds, ⅔ cup candied peel, 2 eggs, a little milk, ½ teaspoon salt.

Method: Sift together flour, baking powder, and salt. Rub in butter; add sugar, seeds, and thinly sliced peel. Add beaten eggs with enough milk to make a light dough. Place in a well-greased tin and bake 1½ hours in a moderate (375°) oven.

Oaten Fruit Loaf

Ingredients: 1 cup Irish steel-cut oatmeal, 2 cups flour, 2 cups white seedless raisins, ½ cup chopped nuts, 3 tablespoons honey, ⅓ cup butter, ⅔ cup milk, 1 egg, 2 teaspoons baking powder, 1 teaspoon salt, 1 cup boiling water.

Method: Add boiling water to oatmeal and let stand not more than 4 hours. (Some people like to cook the oatmeal to porridge consistency. I think this is a mistake—it spoils the characteristic nutty consistency of the true oatmeal loaf.) Sift flour with salt and baking powder. Melt butter and add to oatmeal. Add honey. Combine beaten egg and milk and add alternately with flour to oatmeal mixture. Stir in fruit. Turn into buttered loaf pan and bake 1 hour 10 minutes in a moderate (350°) oven.

Oaten Honey Loaf

Ingredients: 1 cup Irish steel-cut oatmeal, 1 cup boiling water, 2 cups sifted flour, 2 teaspoons baking powder, 1 teaspoon salt, 1 tablespoon honey, 2 tablespoons butter, 1 egg, ⅔ cup milk.

Method: Add boiling water to oatmeal and let stand 4 hours. Sift flour with baking powder and salt. Melt butter and add to oatmeal. Add honey. Beat egg lightly and combine with milk. Add alternately with flour to oatmeal mixture. Turn into buttered loaf pan and bake 50 minutes in a moderate (350°) oven.

Treacle (Molasses) Loaf

Ingredients: 2 cups sifted flour, 4 tablespoons butter, ¼ cup (packed) brown sugar, 6 tablespoons treacle, 2 teaspoons ground ginger, 2 teaspoons baking powder, 1 egg, ½ cup milk, 3 tablespoons sugar.

Method: Mix treacle with milk and warm slightly. Cream butter and sugar and add to the treacle mixture. Sift together flour, baking powder, and ground ginger. Add flour gradually to the creamed mixture, beating well. Then add beaten egg. Pour into greased flat tin lined with wax paper. Bake 1 hour in a moderate oven (375°). When cold, cut in squares and sift sugar on top.

Treacle (Molasses) Fruit Loaf

Ingredients: 3½ cups whole-meal flour, 4 tablespoons butter, 2 teaspoons salt, 1 cup raisins, ¾ package dry yeast, 2 teaspoons sugar, 4 tablespoons treacle, 1 cup boiling water.

Method: Put treacle and butter in a bowl, add the boiling water, stir well, and leave until barely lukewarm. In the meantime, sift flour with salt. Mix the yeast with the sugar. Add the lukewarm treacle mixture and mix with the flour to a soft dough. Cover with a cloth and leave to rise for 1½ hours in a warm place. Turn the dough onto a floured board, add the raisins, and knead well for 4 minutes. Divide in two parts, and place in 2 well-greased tins (they should be not more than half full). Brush with butter, cover, and again leave in a warm place until the dough has almost doubled its bulk. Bake 1 hour in a hot (450°) oven.

Bíonn Blas Milis Ar An mBeagán

(Small things taste sweet)

BOXTY

In the North and West of Ireland, boxty sometimes takes the place of the Halloween barmbrack as a prognosticator of the year's weddings. A ring wrapped in wax paper is mixed in with the batter. And the girls are warned:

> Boxty-on-the-griddle, boxty-on-the-pan,
> If you don't eat boxty, you'll never get your man.

They have another rhyme which dates back to the days of Bonnie Prince Charlie:

> I'll have none of your boxty,
>   I'll have none of your blarney,
> But I'll throw my petticoat over my head
>   And be off with my Royal Charlie.

Boxty-on-the-Griddle

For this recipe I am indebted to Grannie Doyle of Lennox Street, Dublin, who told me, "Now I'll tell you how our boxty bread was baked. My mother took a couple of grated raw potatoes and a skillet of hot mashed potatoes, 3 or 4 good handfuls of flour with a bit of butter rubbed in and a generous grain of salt—all mixed well and rolled out on the board, cut in squares, and baked on a well-greased griddle to the tune of the children singing:

> 'Three pans of boxty, baking all the day,
>   What use is boxty without a cup of tay?'

The children in those days got very little 'tay.' Each one got a nice tin porringer of milk and sat up to the table and ate hot buttered boxty to the fill—and we lived."

Boxty-on-the-Pan

Ingredients: 1 cup each flour, mashed potato, and grated raw potato; 2 teaspoons each baking powder and salt, 2 eggs, milk to mix.

Method: Squeeze the grated raw potato in a cloth to remove as much moisture as possible. Sift the flour with baking powder and salt. Mix all ingredients well together with beaten eggs; add sufficient milk to make a dropping batter. Drop by tablespoons onto a hot buttered frying pan and cook over moderate heat, allowing about 4 minutes each side. Serve hot and well buttered, with or without sugar.

2

Cakes and Cookies

"Thou shalt take also fine flour, and shalt bake twelve loaves thereof..."
Leviticus XXIV, 5

LARGE CAKES

*I*t seems unbelievable that there was a time—and not so very long ago, either—when our village knew nothing of the intricacies of cake-making. Today, if an American visitor were to walk into almost any home in Ballyderrig at teatime she would get a surprise in addition to the traditional welcome. Such a surprise, in fact, that she would wonder if she were not back home in Oshkosh or Brooklyn or Quakertown, or in any of the places to which such American delicacies as pineapple upside-down cake and chocolate cookies are indigenous.

It is Polly Sweeney who must be thanked for teaching Ballyderrig to rise above currant bread.

"I'm home to stay," Polly announced when she came back to us after working for twenty-five years as a cook in the States.

We did not believe her. It was difficult to credit that she would be willing to live in a quiet little place like ours after the grandeur she had known abroad. Polly had certainly grown into a fashionable woman while she was away from us. In church on Sundays, her stylish clothes came between us and our prayers. Ballyderrig seemed to have little to offer such a woman—particularly now that all her own people were dead and gone.

Those who had known her before she went away said that beneath all the style she was the same simple girl who used to keep company with Jimmy Moore, the assistant in Grogan's grocery store. "Wasn't it lucky for her that Jimmy and herself didn't make a match of it?" they said. "Wasn't it the bright day for her when her people packed her off to America instead of letting her have her way, that time she was so set on marrying him? Look at her now—a well-dressed woman with money in the bank. And look at poor Jimmy, still plodding away in the same old job and not a penny better off than the first day he went to work for Ned Grogan."

Not, indeed, that anyone who worked for Ned would be likely to make his fortune. Old Ned had a genius for working the last ounce of energy out of a man. And he paid a small grudging wage.

"Polly must be clapping herself on the back for having had such a lucky escape," was what we all said.

We spoke too soon. The girl was not home more than a month when she and Jimmy were to be seen walking along the bog road in the evenings, holding hands like a pair of children. We noticed that Jimmy had a new firm set to his shoulders, that Polly's face lost the slight hardness it had worn when she first came home, and that her eyes had become bright and happy.

She had been back a bare three months when she bought Humpy Hyland's little shop which had stood empty for years. For an exciting couple of weeks we watched contractors from Kildare working early and late as they slapped on snowy paint, fitted gleaming chromium, and installed glass shelves. All day long, Polly supervised and directed.

In the evening, when his day's work for Ned Grogan was through, Jimmy Moore hurried to join Polly and review the day's progress.

We were not surprised, then, when we heard their banns called. In next to no time Ned Grogan was looking for a new assistant and Ballyderrig had a second grocery store.

Everyone—excepting, of course, Ned—wished them well, but there were quite a few pessimists who thought that Polly would have been wiser to keep her money in the bank. "They'll never make a go of it," said the gloomy prophets. "Jimmy is one of the decentest fellows in Ireland, but there's no denying that he's a stick-in-the-mud. He's not the type to make a success of a business of his own."

They reckoned without Polly. She sat at the cash register while Jimmy sliced and weighed and wrapped and packaged. There was a happy go-ahead air about him that showed he had at last got what he needed: the one woman out of all the world capable of putting life and spirit into him.

But it was not the regeneration of Jimmy that brought custom to the Moores. It was the fact that Polly threw in free with the goods we bought a share of the cooking wisdom she had gathered during her years in America.

"Is that a tin of treacle you are buying?" she would ask. "You ought to try treacle fruit cake sometime."

Or, "Would you ever think of making cookies for a change? The children will love them." And then the recipe would be scribbled out and handed along with your change.

It was no wonder that old Ned Grogan finally had to put up his shutters. We would have been sorry for him if he had had dependents. But Ned had always been too mean to marry, and there was neither chick nor child to suffer when he retired to a hotel in Newbridge.

"Anyway," we said, "why should we have gone on dealing where we got nothing but sour looks and grunts, when the Moores offered us good value, smiles, and a free course in cooking?"

Just the same, in addition to baking Polly's good American cakes, we continued to make the cakes which had been baked by our grand-mothers.

Apple Barmbrack

Ingredients: 4 cups sifted flour, 1 cup sugar, 1 cup raisins, 1 cup white seedless raisins, 1 cup (½ pound) butter, 1½ cups unsweetened apple-sauce, 3 teaspoons baking soda, 1 teaspoon salt.

Method: Sift flour with salt and baking soda. Mix in fruit and sugar. Add applesauce and mix thoroughly. Turn into greased and lined tin and bake 1½ hours in a moderate (350°) oven. This cake will keep fresh for a month.

Christmas Cake (Very Rich)

Ingredients: 2 cups (1 pound) butter, 4 cups sifted flour, 2 cups sugar, 3 cups raisins, 1½ cups chopped orange and lemon peel, ¾ cup candied cherries, ¾ cup blanched almonds, ½ cup ground almonds, 3 cups cur-rants, 2 tablespoons allspice, 8 eggs, 1 teaspoon salt, ½ cup brandy, 1 tablespoon orange-flower water, 1 tablespoon rose water, 2 tablespoons caramel.

Method: To make the caramel, boil 4 tablespoons sugar and 2 of water in a heavy saucepan until the mixture is a good deep brown. Care must be taken not to let the caramel scorch, as the slightest taste of burning will spoil the flavor of the cake. Add the caramel while hot to other liquids.

Sieve together flour, salt, spices, and ground almonds. Pour boiling water over the whole almonds, leave them for five minutes then slip off the skins and shred. Quarter the cherries. Chop the peel and combine with the raisins, currants, shredded almonds, and cherries. Beat the eggs slightly and add to them the brandy, caramel, orange-flower water, and rose water. Warm the butter slightly in a mixing bowl and cream with the sugar; on no account must the butter be allowed to melt beforehand. Add the eggs, a little at a time, and beat thoroughly but lightly into the creamed mixture. Care must be taken in adding the last of the eggs to prevent the mixture from curdling (curdling gives a cake a coarse, pebbly texture). To prevent curdling, add a little of the flour mixture before adding the last of the eggs. Now fold in very lightly the flour mixture. (Flour should never be beaten into a cake mixture or the cake will be tough.) Lastly, stir in the fruit.

Line bottom and sides of a pan 10″ square by 3½″ deep with two thicknesses of wax paper, and tie a double band of brown paper around the outside of the tin. Stand the tin on a large baking sheet (covered with a layer of salt to prevent burning). Put the mixture into the prepared tin and bake 5½ hours in the middle of a moderately slow (300°) oven. Allow the cake to stand on the rack for a few minutes, until it begins to shrink from the sides of the tin. Remove from tin and place on a cake rack until cold. Store in a cool dry place until about 2 weeks before Christmas, when the almond icing may be put on. If an extra-rich cake is desired, now and again during the storing period make a few holes in the top of the cake with a skewer or knitting needle and trickle in a teaspoonful of brandy.

In Ireland we spare neither trouble nor money in beautifying the Cake-of-the-Year. The cake is usually made in late October and left to mellow until a fortnight before Christmas when it gets its thick coating of almond paste. A week later, it is glorified with royal frosting and decorations.

Almond Paste (Marzipan)

Ingredients: 5 cups ground almonds, 3½ cups sifted confectioner's sugar, 1 cup sugar, 4 eggs, juice of 1 lemon, 1 teaspoon vanilla, 1 tablespoon each rum and orange-flower water.

Method: Crush confectioner's sugar with rolling pin and sieve well. Mix dry ingredients. Beat the eggs and add gradually with the flavorings. Mix to a paste, first with a wooden spoon and then with the hand. A word of warning: While it is essential to work the marzipan into a smooth paste, it must not be overhandled or it will become crumbly and brittle and difficult to roll and mold. Having kneaded the paste, wrap it in wax paper, put it in a covered jar or tin, and leave until next day when it will be easier to handle.

To Apply Almond Paste to Christmas Cake:

The cake needs a little special preparation before putting on the almond paste. For best results you need an even surface. If the cake has not risen evenly, remember that with ingredients at their present price every crumb is worth its weight in gold, so do not cut away hunks of the cake. You can always (a) turn the cake upside down, or (b) camouflage any unevenness with almond paste. If, in spite of the precautions taken against burning, the bottom or sides have burnt spots, grate them off with a fine grater.

Brush off any loose crumbs, and then give the cake a coat of slightly beaten egg white or warm jelly or warmed sieved jam, to make the almond paste stick. Knead the paste a little, divide it in two, and on a pastry board sprinkled with sugar roll out one piece into a round large enough to cover the top of the cake. Put the round of paste on the cake, and then run the rolling pin lightly over it to make it even. Now take a piece of string and measure the circumference of your cake. Roll out the paste for the sides in two even pieces (they will be easier to manage than if you try to put on the paste in one long strip). Press the two lengths of paste in position and make the sides smooth and symmetrical by rolling a jam jar or milk bottle around the sides. The cake may now be covered and put away in a dry place for a week, when it will be ready for the royal frosting.

Royal Frosting

1. Don't use lemon juice: it tends to turn frosting yellow.
2. Don't omit to scald thoroughly the bowl in which the frosting is to be made: the slightest trace of grease will spoil its appearance.
3. Don't let a speck of egg yolk into the whites: it would spoil that glossy, pure-white finish.
4. Don't skimp on the beating: royal frosting must be beaten until it becomes smooth and snowy and stiff.
5. Don't use more than the minimum of sugar necessary to get the frosting to the required consistency. Remember that it is light and thorough beating that makes good frosting, not extra sugar.

Ingredients: (Sufficient for a large Christmas Cake) 4 egg whites, 7 cups sifted confectioner's sugar, ¼ teaspoon acetic acid, 3 drops laundry blue.

Method: Place carefully separated egg whites in a bowl. Beat slightly for a minute, just long enough to make them liquid. A wooden spatula will make the beating much easier. If there are any lumps in the confectioner's sugar, crush with a rolling pin over paper, and sieve twice. Allow 4 cups (2 pounds) sifted sugar to four egg whites. Add half of the sugar and beat lightly for about 2 minutes. Add the remainder of the sugar gradually, beating well after each addition. Before the frosting is quite stiff enough add ¼ teaspoon acetic acid. At the last minute—to make sure that the frosting will be as white as the driven snow—beat in 3 drops of ordinary laundry blue. Don't worry if the frosting looks a little too blue; the blueness will disappear in beating and the frosting will dry out quite white. But do not use more than 3 drops of rather weak blue, or the frosting may have a grayish tinge.

To Apply Royal Frosting

Some folks have a special revolving frosting table; otherwise place the cake on an upturned plate and stand this on a solid inverted bowl. Since the frosting, if it is the right consistency, must be so thick that it is liable to dry out quickly keep a damp cloth over the bowl of frosting while you are working. Use a spatula to spread the frosting. Keep a jug of hot water at hand, and dip the spatula into this now and then, shaking well to remove the drops after each dipping. If you are frosting both top and sides of the cake, put the greater part of the frosting on top. Spread it smoothly, then coat the sides, turning the cake around with your left hand as you work. To secure a smooth top, hold the spatula so that the end of the blade is at the center of the cake, and revolve the cake, pressing very lightly on the spatula. Don't lift the spatula off the cake as you finish; draw it lightly toward you and you will avoid leaving a line. Most people are satisfied with one coat of frosting, but I like to add another after the first coat has been allowed to dry out for a day or two. A very smooth top may be obtained by adding a coat of frosting that is almost, but not quite, thick enough to pour. Having put this on top of the cake, lift the plate and give it a few smart taps on the bowl: the frosting should flow perfectly smooth.

For special pastry-tube decorations, the frosting should be stiffer than for coating, but decorating should not be attempted until the frosting proper is quite dry. First select your design, place it over the top of the cake, and then prick it out with a darning needle. For a good effect, do your writing or trellis work with a No. 2 pantry tube in white frosting; when this is dry, go over it with pink frosting, using a No. 1 tube.

N.B.: The above recipe, with appropriate decorations, is also used for the traditional wedding cake.

Farmer's Cake

Ingredients: 4 cups sifted flour, 1½ cups (¾ pound) butter, 1½ cups (firmly packed) brown sugar, 6 eggs, 2 tablespoons allspice, 1 teaspoon grated nutmeg, 1 teaspoon salt, 2 tablespoons lemon juice, 2 teaspoons baking soda, 4 cups raisins, 1 cup chopped peel, 4 cups currants, 1 cup candied cherries, ½ cup whiskey.

Method: Sift flour with salt and spices. Rub butter into mixture. Add sugar, fruit, and peel. Dissolve baking soda in lemon juice and combine with beaten eggs and whiskey. Add liquid to dry ingredients and mix well. Turn into heavy tin, lined with several thicknesses of wax paper. Bake 4½ hours in a moderate (300°) oven.

Gur (or Chester) Cake

I imagine this cake owes its name to the fact that tuppence worth of inferior baker's Chester Cake is the usual provender of boys who are "on gur," *i.e.,* playing hookey. But a grand way to use up stale bread or cake is in making good homemade gur.

Ingredients: ½ recipe for Lardy Cakes (p. 37), 2 cups sifted flour, 2 cups fine cake or bread crumbs, 2 teaspoons baking powder, ½ cup corn syrup (about), 1 cup currants, 1 teaspoon ground ginger, a little beaten egg.

Method: Divide the pastry in two and roll thin. Use half to line the bottom of a greased jelly-roll pan (shallow baking pan about 12″ x 9″). Now sieve flour, baking powder, and ginger. Mix in currants and crumbs. Add corn syrup to make a stiff paste. Mix thoroughly and spread evenly in tin. Cover with remaining pastry. Brush with beaten egg and mark in squares. Bake 40 minutes in a 375° oven. When cold, cut into squares.

Lenten Cake (Eggless)

Ingredients: 4 cups sifted flour, ½ cup (¼ pound) butter, 3 tablespoons molasses, 1 cup milk, ¾ cup sugar, 3 teaspoons allspice, ½ cup raisins, 2 teaspoons baking powder, 1 teaspoon baking soda, ½ teaspoon salt.

Method: Melt butter, add molasses and milk and cool. Sift flour, spice, baking powder, baking soda, and salt. Stir butter mixture into dry ingredients. Add raisins and mix well. Pour into buttered tin and bake 1½ hours in a 350° oven.

Nun's Cake

Ingredients: ¾ cup butter, 1 cup sugar, 3 eggs, 2 tablespoons cornstarch, 4 cups sifted flour, 1 teaspoon vanilla, ½ teaspoon salt, 3 teaspoons baking powder, ½ cup milk, 1 strip citron peel.

Method: Sift flour with cornstarch and baking powder. Cream butter. Add sugar, one tablespoon at a time, beating well. Add beaten eggs one at a time, beating well after each addition. Just before beating in the last egg, sprinkle in a little of the flour mixture. Add vanilla. Fold in dry ingredients alternately with milk. Place strip of citron peel on top. Bake in a greased lined tin for one hour in a moderate (350°) oven. When done let stand 5 minutes in the tin before turning out onto a rack.

Plum Duff

This is a glorified version of Gur Cake.

Ingredients: 4 tablespoons mixed currants, raisins, and chopped orange peel; 8 tablespoons (4 ounces) blanched shredded almonds, 3 cups sifted flour, 2 cups sugar, 3 teaspoons baking powder, 2 teaspoons cinnamon, 1 teaspoon each ground ginger, allspice, and grated nutmeg; 1 cup milk, ½ recipe for Lardy Cakes (p. 37).

Method: Sift flour with spices and baking powder. Combine dry ingredients and mix well. Line a buttered jelly-roll pan with very thin shortcrust pastry. Spread with the fruit mixture and cover with a lid of paper-thin pastry. Brush with beaten egg, prick with a fork, and bake 40 minutes in a moderate (350°) oven. Cut in squares and serve hot or cold.

Porter Cake

Ingredients: 4 cups sifted flour, 1 cup (½ pound) butter, 1 cup sugar, 3 cups raisins, 2 eggs, 1 cup porter or Guinness stout, 2 teaspoons baking powder, 6 tablespoons chopped citrus peel, 1 teaspoon each nutmeg and allspice, 2 teaspoons salt.

Method: Sieve flour, salt, and baking powder; add sugar, nutmeg, and allspice. Rub in butter finely. Add fruit. Add porter or stout mixed with beaten eggs. Bake in a well-greased loaf tin 2 hours in a moderate (375°) oven.

Potato Seedy Cake

Ingredients: 1½ cups sifted flour, 1 cup mashed potato, ½ cup sugar, ½ cup currants, 1 teaspoon salt, ½ teaspoon allspice, 1 teaspoon caraway

seeds, 2 large eggs, 4 tablespoons butter, 2 teaspoons baking powder.
Method: Sift flour with baking powder, salt, and allspice; rub in the
butter. Add caraway seeds. Mix in sugar, currants, and mashed potato.
Mix to a fairly stiff consistency with beaten eggs. Place in a well-greased
flat tin and bake 30 minutes in a 425° oven. Cut into squares and serve hot.

Rink Cake

This cake got its name because it was usually served at a dance for
which the Irish word is *rinnce*.
Ingredients: 1 cup sifted flour, ½ cup sugar, 2 teaspoons baking powder,
2 eggs, ¼ cup butter, 4 tablespoons (2 ounces) almonds (blanched and
chopped), 2 tablespoons currants, ½ teaspoon salt.
Method: Sift together flour, baking powder, and salt. Rub in the butter
and sugar. Mix to a dough with eggs. Place in a well-buttered shallow tin.
Sprinkle the top with the currants and almonds. Bake 20-25 minutes in a
425° oven.

Simnel Cake

Mothering Sunday, the mid-Sunday of Lent, calls for a special cake
for mothers. This pleasant custom dates from the sixteenth century.
In those days girls who had hired themselves as servants at the New
Year hiring fairs were given a holiday in mid-Lent so that they might
visit their families. To prove their cooking skill they brought home a
gift of a "Mothering" or "Simnel" cake. And because the Lenten fast
in those times was rigorous, they used a rich mixture so the cake would
keep until Easter.

As well as this evidence of her newly acquired cooking skill the
girl sometimes brought home for family approval her newly acquired
sweetheart. And, if she happened to be a dairymaid or laundrymaid,
the sweetheart bought or had made for her the Mothering cake. There
is an old verse which goes:

> And I'll to thee a simnel bring
> 'Gainst thou goest a-mothering;

So that when she blesses thee
Half the blessing thou'lst give me.

All my life long I have been reading theories which purported to explain how the simnel cake got its name. One story had it that the father of Lambert Simnel, who was a pretender to the English throne, was the baker and inventor of this cake. The most generally accepted explanation told how a couple called Simon and Nellie could not agree on whether the Mothering cake should be a fruit cake or an almond cake. They finally decided (so the story went) to combine the two, and they insisted that the name of each should be perpetuated—hence Simnel.

Last Lent, all by myself, I discovered the true origin of the name of this grand cake. It occurred to me to look it up in Chambers' dictionary. This is what I found:

Simnel, a sweet cake for Christmas, Easter, or Mothering Sunday (origin: Fr. *simenel,* L. *simila,* fine flour). So much for the name. Now for the cake.

Simnel Cake

Cream together 1 cup (½ pound) butter with 1 cup sugar. Sift 2 cups flour with 1 teaspoon grated nutmeg, 1 teaspoon ground cinnamon, 1 teaspoon ground ginger, ½ teaspoon salt, and 2 teaspoons baking powder. With 2¼ cups raisins and 2 cups currants mix ¾ cup cherries and ¾ cup chopped candied peel. Beat 4 eggs, add 2 tablespoons milk and 1 teaspoon vanilla. Work beaten eggs into creamed mixture. Gradually add half the flour, then add all the fruit, finally mix in remainder of flour. (The cake mixture should be fairly stiff.) Line a 9-inch tin with several thicknesses of wax paper. Put half the mixture into tin, smoothing top evenly. Over this place a ½-inch round of almond paste (p. 29). Add remainder of mixture, smooth top, and bake in a slow (325°) oven for 4 hours. When cake is cool, cut out another round of almond paste exactly the size of cake. Cut a 3-inch round from the center and place the ring of paste on top of cake. Form a number of small balls or eggs (11 is the traditional number) with remainder of paste and lay these at intervals on the ring of almond paste. Brush with beaten egg and place in a hot (500°) oven for 3 minutes or until paste is slightly brown. When cold, fill center of the cake with glacé frosting, and when this is set with a pastry tube write an appropriate inscription ("To Mother," etc.).

Glacé Frosting

1 cup sieved confectioner's sugar, 2 tablespoons water, 1 tablespoon strained lemon juice. Combine ingredients in top of double boiler and stir over hot water until sugar is melted. The frosting should be only warm. While still warm, pour over cake.

COOKIES

Did the cookie come from Ireland?

The first written mention of cookies occurs in the ancient *Book of Lismore.*

It seems that when Saint Patrick came to Ireland he found that Ogham—the only form of writing then known here—was the closely guarded secret of the Druids. Patrick in his wisdom realized that education was a necessary preliminary to conversion from Paganism, and he introduced the Roman alphabet to the people to whom he was bringing the gifts of enlightenment and salvation.

In the *Book of Lismore* we are told that the child who grew up to be Saint Columcille found difficulty in learning the alphabet. To encourage him, his mother baked A-B-C cookies with which he was rewarded as he mastered letter after letter.

It is very probable that this sweet way of coaxing children to learn became common throughout Ireland. And I think it quite likely that it was introduced to America by Saint Brendan the Navigator who discovered the New World long before Columbus set foot there.

Flour kneaded with honey and nuts would have been the basis of those A-B-C biscuits of long ago. Here is a modern version:

Columcille Cookies

Ingredients: 2 cups sifted flour, 1 cup whole meal, 2 teaspoons baking powder, ¾ teaspoon salt, 4 tablespoons butter, 1 egg, milk to mix. For filling: 5 tablespoons honey, 2 tablespoons butter, 3 tablespoons chopped hazelnuts.

Method: Sift dry ingredients, rub in butter. Add beaten egg and sufficient milk to make a soft but nonsticky dough. Turn onto floured board and knead gently. Roll ¼-inch thick and cut in rounds with pastry cutter. Make filling by mixing together honey, butter, and nuts. Spread filling on half of rounds; cover with remaining rounds and press edges together with a fork. Place on a lightly greased baking sheet and bake 20 minutes in a hot (450°) oven.

Fraughan (Blueberry) Muffins

These are a "must" for the third Sunday in July, for it is then that the fraughans—known elsewhere as blueberries—are at their best.

Ingredients: 2 cups sifted flour, 2 teaspoons baking powder, ½ cup sugar, 4 tablespoons soft butter, 1 teaspoon salt, 1 egg, ½ cup milk, 1 cup fraughans.

Method: Sift together dry ingredients. Cut in soft shortening until barely blended. Add fruit. Add unbeaten egg and milk and stir only until ingredients are blended and the flour moistened. The batter should be lumpy. Fill greased muffin tins ⅔ full. Bake 25 minutes in a moderate (400°) oven. Remove immediately from tins, using a sharp knife or spatula. Serve hot.

Lardy Cakes

These are a delicacy associated with pig-killing time when "flead" or leaf lard is plentiful.

Ingredients: 3 cups sifted flour, 1½ cups (¾ pound) leaf lard, 1 teaspoon salt, 1 egg, cold water to mix.

Method: Sieve flour and salt together. Scrape ⅓ of the flead and rub lightly in. Mix to a dough with cold water and roll out on a floured board. Scrape another third of the lard and spread it over the paste in flakes. Fold in three and beat out with the rolling pin. Repeat with remaining lard and beat again. Roll out to ¼-inch thickness, cut in small rounds, brush with beaten egg, and bake 12 minutes in a 450° oven. Eat hot with butter.

N.B.: This makes good shortcrust pastry for pies.

Oat Cakes

Ingredients: 1 cup flake oatmeal, ¾ cup ground oats, ¾ teaspoon salt, 2 tablespoons lard, hot water to mix.

Method: Mix together flake oats, ground oats, and salt. Rub in lard. Add sufficient hot water to make a stiff dough. Knead lightly for a minute or two, then turn out on a board dusted with ground oats. Divide into three parts. Roll each to a round and cut in quarters. Bake 20-25 minutes in a slow (325°) oven, turning the cakes after 15 minutes. When the cakes are done, let stand in a warm place to become thoroughly dry and crisp. Eat well buttered.

Pancakes

Shrove Tuesday pancakes date from the time when the Lenten fast was really rigorous. Every good housewife used up whatever eggs and butter were in her larder by turning them into special cakes on the eve of Ash Wednesday.

So, it is Shrove Tuesday, and the men from the fields tread quick coming in, because they know there will be pancakes for supper—real pancakes, none of your paper-thin rolled foolishness, but good substantial buttermilk pancakes.

There's a platter of them as high as your hip waiting on the hob, with melted butter and sugar trickling down the sides.

What matter if the woman of the house has developed a sprained wrist from beating and mixing and turning pancakes for the past two hours? It's all in a good cause.

Isn't it Pancake Night?

Ingredients: 4 cups sifted flour, 1 teaspoon baking soda, 1 teaspoon salt, 2 eggs, enough buttermilk to make a thick batter, butter and sugar for spreading.

Method: Sift flour with salt and baking soda. Break eggs into a well in center and mix thoroughly. Beat in enough buttermilk to make a thick batter. Drop by spoonfuls onto a greased pan. Butter them as they come from the pan and sprinkle thickly with sugar.

Petticoat Tails

This rather peculiar name is probably a corruption of "petite galette" (little cake).

Ingredients: 4 cups sifted flour, 1¼ cups (½ pound, plus 4 tablespoons) butter, ¾ cup sugar, 1 egg.

Method: Work butter into flour, and mix in sugar. Add beaten egg and mix well. Although the mixture will be dry and crumbly, no other liquid should be added. The paste should be worked well with the hands to make it a cohesive mass. Cut it into four parts and roll each in a round about ⅛-inch thick. In the center of each round stamp a circle with a 2-inch pastry cutter. Cut the outside part into 8 equal segments. Lift carefully with a spatula onto a well-greased baking sheet and bake about 20 minutes in a moderate (350°) oven. They should be very pale brown in color. (This recipe makes lovely shortbread.)

Potato Muffins

Ingredients: 1 cup mashed potatoes (hot), ½ cup milk, 1 egg, 1 cup flour, 1 teaspoon salt, 2 tablespoons melted butter, 2 teaspoons baking powder, ¼ cup sugar.

Method: Sprinkle melted butter on mashed potatoes. Sift dry ingredients and mix with potatoes. Stir in milk by degrees, add beaten egg. Fill greased muffin tins ¾ full. Bake 25 minutes in a 400° oven.

Potato Scones

Ingredients: 2 cups mashed potatoes, 1 cup flour, ½ cup (¼ pound) butter, 1 teaspoon salt, 2 teaspoons baking powder.

Method: Sift flour with baking powder and salt, rub in butter. Incorporate with mashed potato, adding no liquid. Roll out ½-inch thick on floured board. Cut in rounds and bake on a greased griddle, allowing 10 minutes to each side. Or bake 20-25 minutes in a moderate (400°) oven. Split, butter, and serve hot.

3

Pies, Puddings, Desserts

"Thou hast prepared a table before me . . ."
Psalm XXII, 5

*B*ut for the love of cowslips which has ruled me all my life I might never have become acquainted with Mrs. McKey's fruit roll. And Ballyderrig might never have made friends with the occupants of Grange.

Everyone was excited when the McKeys came from Dublin to live in Grange. The old house had stood empty for years. "It will be a good thing to have city people living among us," my mother said. " 'Twill liven us up a bit. Dublin people are great for parties and entertaining."

She couldn't have been more mistaken. The McKeys added little or nothing to Ballyderrig's social life. They arrived in the village on a sidecar hired at Kildare station, the father sitting on one side, the mother and twenty-year-old daughter sitting on the other. There was a bleak look about the three of them that—as things turned out—did not lie.

Never once in the weeks that followed did they give a sign of wanting to have anything to do with us. When Mrs. McKey did her shopping, she walked hurriedly among us with no more than a quiet "good day"—a fragile little woman she was with a harassed air. Mr. McKey was just as aloof on those rare occasions when he came into the place. He was heavy-footed, as if burdened, and his lined face had a grim, shut-in look. The daughter was never seen at all. "She must think herself too good to walk on the same street as country people" was our comment.

Grange has always been a great place for cowslips. The big old chestnut trees which paraded the avenue held warmth in their roots, and the donkey-brown branches dripped moisture to soften the earth and coax up the cowslips long before they appeared anywhere else. While Grange had stood empty we children had made our own of the cowslips, but the coming of the McKeys created difficulties.

"You keep far away from Grange," my mother warned me. "They'll only run you. The McKeys don't want us. And maybe we don't want them."

For my birthday that year (I was born in May) I had been given a Red Ridinghood doll. Her lovely clothes could be taken off. Every garment down to the little lace-edged panties had tapes and buttons. On the day after my birthday I took the doll down to the Laughlins to show her to my friend Mary Jo.

My way led past Grange. I looked in through the gate. What I saw sent my mother's warning out of my head. Every chestnut tree stood in a golden ring of cowslips. I pushed open the gate. Leaving my doll sleeping in a mossy cleft between the great roots, I bent to pick. The stems were as smooth and cool as I had known they would be, and every nod of the gentle fringed heads released the loveliest smell in the world.

And then I heard voices right beside me. I jumped and turned. Mrs. McKey and her daughter were standing there. The young woman had my Red Ridinghood doll in her arms. She was hugging it to her and resisting all her mother's attempts to take it from her.

"Come on, Annie," the mother urged. Her face was the saddest I had ever seen. "Give the little girl her doll. I'll get you another."

My seven-year-old sense of importance was flattered that a grownup should wish to play with my doll. How was I to know that twenty-year-old Annie's mind had stopped growing when she was five? "She can play with it for a little while," I conceded.

Mrs. McKey hesitated. "Come into the house, then," she said. "It's teatime." She gave us tea, a lovely tea. There was fruit roll and an apple flan in which the apples were a lovely red. I learned afterward that she managed this by cooking a few slices of beets with the apples. When the tea was over Annie and Mr. McKey and I played tiddly-winks. I found that he was not grim at all—only quiet and kind.

When it was time for me to go home Annie cried because I was taking away my doll, and I had to promise to come back the next day.

I told my mother about my afternoon. As she listened her face grew almost as sad as Mrs. McKey's. "May heaven comfort them," she said. "So that's what's wrong!" She had a great kindness and a great understanding, my mother. That night she did not go to bed until all hours. When I went to Grange next day I had a present for Annie from my mother—a doll dressed in even lovelier clothes than my Red Ridinghood.

That was the start of a great friendship between the McKeys and the people of Ballyderrig. Annie was never lonely again. There was always children who were glad to play at Grange—as much, I honestly believe, out of liking for Annie as out of appreciation of the lovely teas Mrs. McKey gave us. And when, a couple of years later, the flu epidemic took the overgrown child to Heaven, we were still made welcome at Grange. Mrs. McKey cooked nothing that we liked better than the rich spicy fruit roll. Easy to make, it was, too. Just an oblong of shortcrust pastry (use ¼ recipe Apple Cake pastry, p. 43) brushed with melted butter and covered with a layer of chopped raisins, nuts, candied peel, and apples, sweetened with a sprinkling of brown sugar, and enlivened with a dusting of cinnamon. Wet the edges, roll up, and bake 45 minutes in a moderate (375°) oven.

Apple Cake

I doubt if the ancient Irish ever had such good pastry as this. Even today the traditional apple cake is a rather heavy affair. Long ago their greatest delicacies in the way of pastry were cakes kneaded with honey or with salmon roe. Their dessert would have been oatcakes dipped in honey with hazelnuts and apples. But we like to have apple cake on the menu as a tribute to one of Patrick's disciples, Saint Columba. One of his deeds was the blessing of the sour apples at Durrow and the immediate sweetening of them.

Ingredients: 4 cups flour, 2 cups (1 pound) shortening, 1 cup sugar, 1 pinch salt, grated peel of 1 lemon, 4 eggs, milk as needed to make dough of a consistency to roll, 1 No. 3 can (about 5¾ cups) applesauce, ½ teaspoon cinnamon, 1 pinch ground cloves, whipped cream.

Method: Blend flour, shortening, sugar, salt, grated lemon peel, and the lightly beaten eggs. Add milk as required, roll ½-inch thick, and line pie pan.

Mix the applesauce with the cinnamon and cloves, spread over dough in pie pan, and top with dough rolled to ½-inch thickness. Bake 1 hour in moderate (375°) oven. Serve in deep dish with whipped cream.

Apple Pratie

The traditional Irish pratie, which is a feature of Halloween in some districts in the North and West, is, I am afraid, rather heavy for the taste of most people. It is made with potato pastry about 1-inch thick. I prefer the following individual potato apple cakes. Make a dough as for ordinary potato cakes (p. 33). The dough should be rolled thin (about ¼-inch). Cut it in rounds, and between each two rounds sandwich chopped apples. Bake in the oven till brown. The tops can then be removed and sugar sprinkled on the apples to taste. Some people like to add wee scraps of butter as well. The tops are then replaced, and the apple pratie returned to the oven for a minute or two for the sugar and butter to melt. Or they can be served straightway. It is better to add the sugar after the cakes are cooked, otherwise the melting sugar is inclined to make the underhalf of the scone rather soggy.

Apple Puddeny-Pie

Ingredients: 4 medium cooking apples, 1 teaspoon cinnamon, ½ teaspoon nutmeg, 2 teaspoons lemon juice, ½ teaspoon baking soda, ½ cup sugar, 1 cup flake oatmeal, ⅓ cup butter, 1 teaspoon grated lemon rind, ⅓ cup water.

Method: Pare and core apples. Cut in eighths and place in greased baking dish. Sprinkle with combined spices. Add water, lemon juice, grated rind, and sugar. Add baking soda to flake oatmeal and work butter into this mixture until crumbly. Spread oatmeal mixture over apples and bake 40 minutes in a moderate (375°) oven.

Carrageen Mold

The edible sea moss of Ireland is good for health, complexion, and hair. Mrs. Mary Sweeney of Donegal who celebrated her 103rd birthday on December 13, 1959, told me that she had vivid memories of the post-Famine days when people managed to keep alive on carrageen porridge. Today we have a more delectable way of cooking this valuable food.

Ingredients: 1 cup carrageen, 3 tablespoons sugar, 2 teaspoons vanilla, 1 teaspoon salt, 4 cups milk. For decoration: whipped cream and citron peel, or green gelatine made according to directions on box.

Method: Wash the moss and steep 15 minutes in cold water. Drain well. Tie it loosely in muslin. Put it in the top of a double boiler with the milk and salt. Cook until a spoonful will set when poured on a cold saucer. Stir in the sugar. Strain and add vanilla. Pour into a rinsed mold. When set, turn out and decorate with whipped cream and citron peel, or with green gelatine set on a flat dish and cut into shamrocks.

Christmas Pudding

Ingredients: 4 cups (1 pound) breadcrumbs, 2 cups each raisins and currants; 2 cups finely chopped beef suet, ½ cup ground almonds, 2 tablespoons allspice, 1 teaspoon salt, 6 eggs, 2 tablespoons brandy, juice and grated rind of 2 medium lemons, 3 tablespoons blanched and shredded almonds, 1 teaspoon grated nutmeg, 1 cup dried chopped figs,

4 tablespoons each chopped candied orange, citron, and lemon peel; 1 cup cider, 1 cup brown sugar.

Method: Mix together suet, spices, and ground almonds. Stir in fruit, peel, lemon rind, and shredded almonds. Soak crumbs in cider 10 minutes. Beat sugar into well-beaten eggs. Add lemon juice, brandy, cider and soaked crumbs. Stir into fruit mixture and beat well. Turn into 3 well-buttered 2-pound (1 quart) bowls, tie down with several thicknesses of greased brown paper and steam 3½ hours. When cold, tie down with fresh paper, store in a cool dry place. They will keep for months. On the day the puddings are to be eaten, steam for 2 hours. During the steaming it is important to keep a kettle of water boiling so as to renew the water in the pot when necessary. The water should not come more than three-quarters up the sides of the bowl.

To Serve: Turn the pudding onto a hot dish. Stick a sprig of berried holly on top. Pour ½ cup Irish whiskey over the pudding and set it alight just before serving. Serve hard sauce separately.

Just for luck, each member of the family—and any friends who happen to drop in while the pudding is being mixed—should give a stir or two to the mixture. In Ireland we like to make three puddings—one for Christmas Day, one for New Year's Day, and one for Twelfth Day.

Mince Pie

Before Cromwell and his Puritans descended like a plague on Ireland our Christmas mince pies were made in cradle-shaped tins in memory of the Christ Child's Manger. And the spices which enlivened the filling were a commemoration of the gifts of the Three Wise Men.

Cromwell banned the mince pie in all its forms, condemning it as "Papish and idolatrous." Cromwell could have saved his breath to cool his porridge. After four hundred years we Irish continue to eat our mince pies while Oliver Cromwell looks on in helpless chagrin from whatever niche he occupies in the nether regions.

Filling for Mince Pie:

2 cups finely chopped beef suet, 2 cups chopped apples, 3 cups currants, 2 cups raisins, 2 cups chopped mixed candied peel, 1 teaspoon each salt, grated nutmeg, ground ginger, and allspice; juice and grated rind of 3

lemons, ½ cup brandy, ½ cup port wine. Mix all ingredients well together and tie down with wax paper dipped in brandy.

To make Mince Pie:

Line pie pan with thiny rolled good puff pastry (see below). Fill with mincemeat. Dampen edge of pastry and cover with a lid of paste. Brush with beaten egg taking care not to let egg go over edge of pie (this would keep the pastry from puffing). Bake 12 minutes in a hot (450°) oven.

Puff Pastry

Ingredients: 2 cups (1 pound) butter (unsalted is best), 3 cups sifted flour, 1¼ cups ice water.

Method: Rub 1 tablespoon of butter into flour and mix to a dough with ice water. Knead 5 minutes on a lightly floured board, cover with cloth and leave 5 minutes. Roll dough to an oblong ½-inch thick. Pat butter to an oblong ½-inch thick and place in center of one side of paste. Fold other side of paste over butter and press edges firmly together. Cover with a cloth and leave 15 minutes. Now fold the oblong of paste in 3, and roll slowly and carefully to an oblong ¼-inch thick. Fold again in 3 and roll slowly and carefully to ¼-inch thick. Fold in 3 to form a square, cover well with cloth or foil, and leave for 2 hours. Roll the paste as before to ¼-inch thickness, fold in 3 and leave, covered, another 2 hours. It may now be rolled to required thickness (¼-inch as a rule) and used.

Potato Fritters

Ingredients: 2 cups riced potatoes, 4 egg yolks, 3 egg whites, 2 tablespoons cream, 2 tablespoons Madeira wine, 2 tablespoons sugar, 1 teaspoon lemon juice, ½ teaspoon nutmeg.

Method: Combine all ingredients and beat 15 minutes or until very light. Drop by spoonfuls into deep boiling fat and fry golden brown (about 6 minutes). Drain on paper towel. Serve with a sauce made by combining 2 tablespoons melted butter, 2 tablespoons sugar, 2 teaspoons lemon juice, and ½ cup Madeira wine.

Rhubarb Flummery

Ingredients: 1 pound (3 cups diced) rhubarb, 6 tablespoons sugar,

1 package raspberry gelatine, 2 eggs, ½ cup whipping cream, 2 tablespoons water.

Method: Simmer rhubarb until tender with 3 tablespoons sugar and the water. Reserve some unbroken pieces for decoration. Put remainder through a sieve. Measure and add sufficient hot water to make up 2 cups. Dissolve gelatine in this. Separate eggs. Whip yolks with remainder of sugar. Stir into rhubarb mixture. When cold, but not set, fold in stiffly beaten egg whites. Pour into custard glasses and decorate with whipped cream and rhubarb.

Tipsy Pudding

Ingredients: ¾ cup sifted flour, ½ cup sugar, 3 eggs, 4 tablespoons rum, 2 tablespoons shredded coconut.

Method: Beat eggs and sugar together until thick and lemon-colored. Fold in flour lightly. Coat 6 well-buttered muffin tins thickly with fine sugar; three quarters fill with mixture. Bake 20 minutes in a moderate (375°) oven. When done, baste with rum sweetened to taste and sprinkle with shredded coconut.

Whiskey Pie

Ingredients: 1 cup milk, 1 strip lemon peel, ½ cup breadcrumbs, 3 tablespoons sugar, 2 eggs, 4 tablespoons butter, 2 tablespoons whiskey, ⅛ recipe Apple Cake pastry (p. 43), 3 tablespoons black currant jam.

Method: Boil lemon peel in milk and pour over breadcrumbs. Let stand 10 minutes, then remove peel. Separate eggs and beat the yolks into the crumb mixture; add melted butter, 2 tablespoons sugar, and whiskey. Roll shortcrust pastry thin, line a 9-inch pie plate, and decorate with a fluted edge. Spread the jam over the pastry, cover with crumb mixture, and bake 45 minutes in a 350° oven. Beat egg whites stiff with remaining sugar, heap on the pie and return to oven until meringue is golden brown.

N.B.: This pie is good eaten cold.

4

Soups

Give we of this red pottage . . .
Genesis, XXV, 30

I wish those magazine writers who lay down rules for happy marriages could have known the Dalys. Brigid was ten years older than Tom. She was an educated woman, a teacher, and the daughter of a teacher. Tom was a weedy product of the Dublin slums, who had spent four years in a reformatory. They never had a family. In spite of all this they were the happiest married couple I have ever known.

It may have been because they possessed something which the know-all writers sometimes overlook. Brigid and Tom Daly had the thing which laughs at writers as well as at locksmiths. They had love. In addition, Brigid was a good cook.

Until she came as teacher to Dunlaney National School, few in our place had any idea of the value of herbs and garlic in cooking. But we began to take interest after hearing Brigid speak at a meeting of the Countrywomen's Association on what a tablespoonful of chives could do for an omelette, and on what a sprig of marjoram and a bay leaf could do for a stew. And when we had visited her lonely little house at Dunlaney bog and had sampled the proof of her words, we all started to spade and to clear handkerchief-sized plots for herb gardens.

The story of Tom and Brigid's meeting and courtship would make a book. She said herself that her patron saint must have had a hand in it, because it all started on St. Brigid's Day.

She had invited me out to supper. "We'll have mutton broth," she promised. It was a raw afternoon for the two-mile walk to Dunlaney, but I knew there would be comfort at the end of it.

Brigid's mutton broth was very special. Instead of using a sheep's head, as the rest of us did, she used lean mutton, diced small. There was eating and drinking on the broth. As you ate, it wasn't just zesty soup you spooned. Each mouthful held as well the delight of tender meat, satisfying barley, and succulent vegetables. The faint incense of onion, parsley, thyme, and bay leaf which hovered over the lovely brew made the name "mutton broth" almost sacrilegious. Eaten with fingers of toast, it made a complete meal.

As I hurried up the garden path to Brigid's front door, the fragrance of my supper came to greet me, making my mouth water.

I got no broth that night. When I went into the kitchen the last of it was being spooned up by a pale, undersized lad of sixteen or so, while Brigid looked on happily.

"This is Tom Daly," she introduced.

The boy got to his feet. "I'd better be going now," he said awkwardly.

"Are you sure you've eaten enough?" Brigid inquired with kindness. That was the most noticeable thing about the dark-haired, dark-eyed Brigid. There was kindness in every comfortable line of her.

"It was grand, thanks," the boy stammered. "I'm full up."

"The bus passes below at the turn, then," she told him. She handed him a ten-shilling note. "Here's your fare. I know that you'll keep your word and go straight back. That you won't let me down."

"I won't," he promised. His heart was shining in his eyes. "I—I won't ever forget you. Good-by—and thanks."

"Who was he, anyway?" I asked, when he had gone.

"He's an unfortunate lad who ran away from Murraystown Reformatory," she told me as she busied herself clearing the table. "I found him here when I came in from school. He broke into the house to look for something to eat. He was starved, the creature, after walking twenty miles across the bog. It was lucky I had the mutton broth ready."

That was Brigid all over. Where another would have given the intending thief a blow, Brigid gave him a meal.

"He was full of fight at first," she said. "But when he saw I was sorry for him he stopped being tough, and showed himself to be only a little boy in trouble. By degrees I got the whole story out of him— the drunken father, the stepmother who didn't want him, and money he stole to go to the pictures. Such a job as I had persuading him to go back!"

"And do you really think he'll go back?" I asked.

"I wish I was as sure of Heaven," she said. "I know children. Something about that boy told me he won't break his word. The poor child!"

Remembering the look he had given her as he went out the door, I could not help thinking that, whatever his age, there was more man than child in Tom Daly.

She reached for the egg bowl. "I'm afraid it will have to be just an omelette," she apologized. "Do you mind?" Under the circumstances I did not mind in the least.

As he had promised, Tom Daly did not forget Brigid. When his time at Murraystown was finished, he came back to Dunlaney. Mrs. Derrigan gave him a job as yard boy. He never looked back. From one job to another he went, bettering himself each time. When he was twenty and earning £3 a week in Logan's garage, Brigid and he started to keep company. When at twenty-five he got his good post in the briquette factory, they were married.

And it all goes to prove that, though the smell of French scent may attract a man, the smell of good, honest broth will anchor him forever.

Brigid's Broth

Ingredients: 2 pounds lean mutton, 4 tablespoons barley (soaked overnight in cold water), 4 tablespoons each chopped carrot, turnip, onion, celery, and cabbage; 2 chopped leeks, 2 tablespoons butter, pepper and salt to taste, 1 tablespoon chopped parsley, 5 cups cold water.

Method: Cut the mutton in ½-inch cubes, season and cover with cold water; bring quickly to boiling point, skim, and add the barley; simmer 1½ hours, or until the meat is tender. Fry the diced vegetables in butter for five minutes without browning. Add to soup with salt and pepper to taste and continue cooking until vegetables are tender. Finally, add the parsley. Shin of beef may be treated this way, too, to make a very good broth, known as Hough Soup. Use 6 tablespoons of rice instead of the barley.

Brothchán Buidhe

This is pronounced "Brohawn Bwee" and it means Yellow Broth. A savory concoction of vegetable stock, thickened with oatmeal and enriched with milk, Brothchán Buidhe was the favorite potage of St. Columba.

There is a story that when Lent came around the saint decided to mortify himself with ersatz broth, so he instructed his cook to put nothing into the broth-pot except water and nettles, with a taste of salt on Sundays.

"Is nothing else to go into it, your Reverence?" asked the cook in horror. "Nothing except what comes out of the potstick," the saint replied sternly.

This went on for two weeks. The saint grew thinner and weaker, and the cook grew more and more worried. And then, all of a sudden, St. Columba started to put on weight again and the worried look left the cook's face. The devoted lay brother had made himself a hollow potstick down which he poured milk and oatmeal. Thus he was able to preserve his master from starvation and himself from the horrible sins of disobedience and lies.

When questioned by the saint he was able to assure him honestly that nothing went into the broth save what came out of the potstick.

Here is the glorified version of Brothchán Buidhe.

Ingredients: 4 cups chicken stock, 4 tablespoons butter, ¼ cup flour, 2 tablespoons flake oatmeal, 1 medium onion, 1 stalk celery, 1 small carrot, 1¾ cups spinach, 2 tablespoons cream, pepper and salt to taste, 1 tablespoon parsley.

Method: To stock add chopped celery, onion, carrot, and salt and pepper to taste. Cook 30 minutes. Knead butter and flour together and add to stock. Sprinkle in oatmeal and add chopped spinach. Simmer 15 minutes. Pass through a sieve, correct seasoning, stir in cream. Sprinkle with minced parsley.

Consommé Befinn

Maybe consommé by any other name would taste as good, but this clear soup *is* rather special. It is full of the zest of ham and beef and vegetable juices. This particular soup inherits its name from a famous heroine in Irish mythology. The reason we connect the lady with ham is this: When King Midir was cajoling her to accompany him to Tír na n-Óg, the Land of the Young, he promised her, among other things, that she should feed on unlimited supplies of pork.

> O lady, if thou comest to my valiant people,
>   A diadem of gold shall be on thy head;
> Flesh of swine, all fresh, banquets of new milk and all
>   Shalt thou have with me there.

> (O'CURRY: *Book of the Dun Cow*)

Ingredients: For stock: 1 ham bone, 1 beef shin bone, 2 medium onions, 4 outside stalks of celery, 2 medium carrots, 1 teaspoon allspice. For garnish: 6 tablespoons each of ham, carrots, and celery cut in julienne strips; 1 tablespoon chopped parsley. Salt and pepper to taste.

Method: Place all stock ingredients in pot, cover with water and simmer three hours. Season to taste with salt and pepper. Garnish each bowl with strips of ham, carrots, and celery just before serving. Sprinkle with parsley.

Cock-a-Leekie Soup

When the Scottish planters came over the border and took over the rich Ulster farms, ordering their rightful owners "to Hell or to Connaught," they brought with them just one good thing: their cock-a-leekie soup.

Ingredients: 1 elderly fowl, 4 pounds shin beef, 3 dozen leeks, 1 cup dried prunes, 1 teaspoon pepper, 2 teaspoons salt, 16 cups (4 quarts) cold water.

Method: Truss the fowl as for boiling. Cut up the beef in small pieces. Wash the leeks, cut in thin slices, using as much as possible of the green part. Put all ingredients, except prunes, into a large pot. Simmer 4 hours, then add stoned prunes and simmer 1 hour longer. Take up the fowl, remove skin, gristle and bones; chop the meat small and return to the pot. Take up the beef, removing stringy portions, chop the rest small and return to the soup. Correct seasoning. The prunes should be left in the soup.

Curragh Soup

Ingredients: 2 tablespoons bacon fat or butter, 4 tablespoons each chopped carrots, onion, and celery; 2 tablespoons chopped leeks, 6 cups (3 pints) boiling water, ½ bay leaf, 2 cups finely chopped cabbage, 4 tablespoons diced raw potato, 4 tablespoons chopped skinned tomato, 1 clove garlic crushed, 2 teaspoons salt, 2 tablespoons grated cheese.

Method: Heat butter or bacon fat in a large stewpan. Add coarsely chopped carrot, onion, celery, and leek. Cook over low heat until the vegetables barely begin to color, stirring and shaking occasionally. Add boiling water. Add salt, bay leaf, and chopped cabbage. Cover and simmer 40 minutes. Add diced potato and simmer another 10 minutes. Now add skinned and chopped tomato, crushed garlic, and parsley. Simmer another 10 minutes. Serve with a sprinkling of grated cheese on each plateful.

Dublin Mussel Soup

Ingredients: 3 pounds (4 pints) mussels, 1 onion, 1 sprig parsley, ¼ cup butter, ½ cup flour, 2 leeks, 1 stalk celery, 4 cups (1 quart) milk, 2 tablespoons cream, ½ teaspoon grated nutmeg, ½ teaspoon pepper, 2 teaspoons salt, ½ cup cider.

Method: Place washed mussels in a saucepan with chopped onion and parsley. Add cider. Cover and place over moderate heat. Shake the saucepan frequently. Remove from heat as soon as mussels open. Strain through a fine cloth, reserving the liquor. With scissors remove beards and place mussels on each side. Melt the butter, add the finely chopped leeks and celery, and sauté for 3 minutes (without browning). Stir in scalded milk; add pepper, salt, and nutmeg and simmer 20 minutes. Pass through a sieve, add liquor from mussels, cream, and then mussels. Reheat to serving point.

Good Friday Soup

For each person, fry 1 sliced medium onion light brown in butter in a heavy stewpan. Add 1 tablespoon flour for each person and stir with a wooden spoon over moderate heat until light brown. Add hot vegetable stock (1 cup for each person) and stir until soup is smooth and thick. Season to taste with pepper and salt. Place 3 or 4 very thin slices of cheese in the bottom of the tureen and pour on the soup. Serve with dry toast.

Kilkenny Leek Broth

Ingredients: 6 medium potatoes, 6 leeks, 4 tablespoons butter or bacon fat, 2 thick slices bread, 6 tablespoons rice, 8 cups (2 quarts) white stock, pepper and salt to taste.

Method: Pare and quarter the potatoes and put to cook with the stock. Slice the leeks and fry with the diced bread in butter or bacon fat until all the fat is absorbed. Add to the potatoes and stock and simmer 30 minutes. Now add the rice and cook 20 minutes longer. Season well with pepper and salt.

Nettle Soup

For many a long year nettles were to the Irish what spinach is to other peoples. And many of us still feel that young tender nettles more than equal the best of spinach. "One feed of nettles in the spring will keep you healthy for the year" is a belief which persists in country parts where the blood-purifying qualities of nettles are still appreciated.

Ingredients: 6 cups (tightly packed) chopped nettle leaves, 2 medium onions, 4 tablespoons butter, 3 cups white stock, 3 cups milk, 4 tablespoons flake oatmeal, 1 leek (chopped). For seasoning: 2 teaspoons salt, 1 teaspoon pepper, ½ teaspoon grated nutmeg. For binding: 1 egg yolk and ½ cup medium cream.

Method: Melt butter in a heavy stewpan over moderate heat. Sauté the chopped onion in the fat (without browning), add nettles and chopped leek. Stir in flake oatmeal. Add combined stock and milk and simmer 50 minutes. Remove from heat and stir in egg yolk beaten with cream. Add seasoning, reheat but do not allow the soup to boil.

Potato Soup

Ingredients: 8 medium potatoes, 3 cups potato water, 1 egg, 2 medium onions, 2 tablespoons butter, 1 cup unsweetened evaporated milk, 2 teaspoons salt, ¼ teaspoon nutmeg, 1 teaspoon pepper, parsley.

Method: Pare and dice potatoes and cook in water to cover until tender; drain and reserve 3 cups of the water. Put the potatoes through sieve or ricer. Mince onions, sauté in butter until slightly browned. Add with seasonings and potatoes to potato water; then add slightly beaten egg, evaporated milk, and nutmeg. Heat, but do not allow to boil, stirring constantly. Garnish with chopped parsley.

Pride of Erin Soup

Ingredients: 1 green cabbage weighing about 1 pound, 2 tablespoons butter, 4 tablespoons chopped raw potato, 3 tablespoons chopped onion, ½ teaspoon ground mace, salt and pepper to taste, 1½ tablespoons flour, 2½ cups milk, 2½ cups water or white stock, 2 tablespoons chopped parsley, 2 tablespoons grated cheese (Parmesan preferably), ¼ cup cream.

Method: Quarter the cabbage, cut away the hard stalk. Cover with boiling water and leave 5 minutes. Drain, pat dry, and shred. Melt the butter in a heavy pan over low heat and simmer the chopped onion until tender, but without browning. Add cabbage and potato and stir over low heat. Add mace, salt, and pepper. Stir in the flour to coat all ingredients, but do not brown. Add the liquid, bring to a boil, and simmer 20 minutes, or until vegetables are tender. Rub through a sieve. Reheat, correct seasoning. If soup is too thick add a little boiling milk. Serve with a spoonful of whipped cream on each serving. Sprinkle parsley and grated cheese on the cream.

Shannon Eel Soup

For generations the people who live on the islands in the Shannon where it widens beyond Athlone have made a good living by supplying London with eels for those jellied eels which the Cockneys love. Now and again they keep some of the eels for making into a good soup.

Ingredients: 2 pounds eels, ¼ cup butter, ½ cup flour, 6 cups water or stock, 1 teaspoon ground mace, a bouquet garni, 1 onion, 3 peppercorns, 1 teaspoon salt, 1 cup vermicelli.

Method: Skin and clean eels and cut them into 2-inch pieces. Combine stock, eels, chopped onion, herbs, peppercorns, and salt and simmer 45 minutes. Strain through a cloth or fine sieve. Melt the butter over gentle heat, stir in flour, blend until it forms a rather dry paste but without browning. Gradually stir in fish liquor and bring to a boil. Sprinkle in vermicelli and cook 4 minutes.

Watercress Soup

Ingredients: 3 cups mashed potatoes, 2 teaspoons salt, 3 cups milk, 2 cups chopped watercress leaves, 2 tablespoons butter.

Method: Combine boiling milk, mashed potatoes, and salt. Stir until smooth and boiling. Add watercress and cook 5 minutes. Remove from heat and stir in butter.

5

Fish

"He said: Have you here any thing to eat? And they offered Him a piece of a broiled fish ..."

Luke XXIV, 41, 42

*F*or proof of what a good fish dinner can do for romance there is no need to look further than Barney Malone.

Barney was a sore thorn in the side of our Fishery Board. From February to August not a salmon in the river was safe from him. The Board had never been able to pin anything on Barney. But in a small place like ours no lawbreaker can hide his misdeeds.

Barney could not have been called a poacher in the ordinary sense. Never in a million years would he have descended to the depravity of using a net. And as for killing a female salmon during the spawning season—well, that was an iniquity no one could have laid at Barney's door. He was a decent and a likable lad. But, there it was: he was the victim of some mysterious compulsion which impelled him irresistibly toward salmon.

Barney might be walking along the riverbank dressed in his best on a Sunday evening. He might be thinking of the wrongs of Ireland, or of the red hair of Nellie Ryan, or of the way Nellie's father opposed their match because Barney would not stay in a steady job. He might be musing on anything under the sun except fish. But the minute he would hear a splash or see a silver gleam, into the water with him, Sunday clothes and all. Out with his gaff then, and in next to no time the river would be one salmon less, and Barney's craving would have found temporary appeasement.

"It's a mania with him," Mr. Hennessy of the Fishery Board often said. "The river draws him the way the public house draws other men. But a stop will have to be put to his gallop. The first time we catch him, he'll go to jail."

The question was: who was going to catch him?

That was the problem bothering Mr. Hennessy as he walked along the road one evening. Old Sam Wheeler, who had been water bailiff for forty years, was due to be retired. *If only we could get the right kind of man to replace him!* Mr. Hennessy mused wistfully. The right kind of active energetic man, a man who'd catch Malone with a salmon.

He came to the cottage where Barney's girl lived with her father, Thatcher Ryan. He stopped and looked at the neat little house with its whitewashed walls and shining new thatch.

Isn't Malone the young fool? he marveled. *There's that grand little girl, and she's mad about him. There's a lovely home waiting for him to hang up his hat in, if only he'd give up the poaching and get himself a steady job. There's no doubt he needs a spell in jail. It would teach him a lesson.*

All of a sudden Mr. Hennessy's nostrils twitched. Through the open window of the cottage was wafted a delicious smell of salmon frying in butter.

Mr. Hennessy crept nearer the window. In a pan on the fire, two thick and rosy salmon steaks sizzled tunefully. The poacher himself was there, sitting comfortably back in his chair. With as carefree an air as if the salmon had been caught legally, Barney looked on while his girl cooked the fish.

Mr. Hennessy threw open the door and walked in. "Caught at last, Malone!" he said. A legacy of ten thousand pounds would not have given him greater glee. "It's the jail for you, my lad."

Barney took it gamely. "Fair enough, Mr. Hennessy." He threw one leg over the other, and his face took on a happily reminiscent look. "Anyway," he said, "I had a good run for my money."

Nellie was not equipped with her lover's fortitude. She burst into tears. Through her sobs she let Mr. Hennessy know that this meant the end of her romance, that her father had sworn that Barney would never put a wedding ring on her finger if the boy ever saw the inside of a jail. She wept and entreated and begged. And the more she wept the greater grew Mr. Hennessy's embarrassment.

Even the chairman of a Fishery Board may have a flesh-and-blood heart. Even a stern official may have sufficient ordinary humanity to sympathize with the distractions of a young and pretty girl who is in love, and who sees her loved one in danger of being whipped away from her. Mr. Hennessy was in a difficult position. There he was with the responsibility on him of ruining the happiness of two young people. At the same time he was a conscientious and a serious-minded man. He had to remember his duty to the Board. "I see no way out of it," he said gruffly. "The whole country knows that Malone has been asking for jail ever since he was old enough to handle a gaff."

Nellie stifled her sobs and dried her eyes. "Since you're here and since it's ready, wouldn't you have a bite to eat, Mr. Hennessy?" Her voice was small and forlorn. "My share of the supper will be thrown out if you don't take it, for I'm that upset this minute I couldn't touch it for all the gold in Ireland."

The suggestion made Mr. Hennessy rear back in horror. How could she imagine that he, the chairman of the Fishery Board, would share such a repast? "Have sense, girl," he grunted, reaching with the tongs for a glowing coal to light his pipe.

For some reason his pipe refused to draw for him and he had to

put it back in his pocket. Maybe the way his mouth was watering was
to blame. No living man could have savored tobacco while watching
Nellie Ryan dish up that meal.

Looking pathetically sad and subdued, she slithered the browned
and buttery steaks onto hot plates. To the north and south of each
steak she spooned little onions and baby carrots that had simmered
in cream. At the east and west she placed mealy boiled potatoes. "Let
it be wasted if it must," she lamented resignedly, as she put the
steaming plates on the table and filled two blue-ringed mugs with
fresh buttermilk. "I'm so demented this minute that I'd choke if I
tried to swallow the smallest little mouthful." She sighed in a way that
wrung Mr. Hennessy's heart. "I'll leave you now while I try to work
some of the desperation out of myself by getting in the fowl for the
night."

Barney Malone felt no qualms about doing justice to that supper.
He pulled his chair to the table. "Even a murderer," said he, "is
allowed a good feed before he goes to the gallows. Since you're send-
ing me to jail, this will likely be the last decent feed I'll be getting for
a while."

He set to. Mr. Hennessy averted his eyes. He began to be very
conscious of the fact that he had not eaten since midday.

"There's no doubt that Nellie is a prize cook," Barney commented.
"This bit of salmon is done to a turn. And I always say that nothing
goes so well with salmon as young vegetables done in cream the way
Nellie cooks them."

Mr. Hennessy swallowed. "It does seem a pity to throw out that
second plateful," he said weakly. "When you think of the starving
people in India it seems a mortal sin to waste anything in the line of
food."

"A deadly sin," Barney agreed. "Sit in to the table, man, while it's
still fit to eat."

Mr. Hennessy sat in. For ten blissful minutes there was no sound
save the satisfying symphony of cutlery and delft.

When Mr. Hennessy finally pushed away his empty plate he knew that warm glow of benevolence which always results from a satisfactory gastronomic experience.

"You're the world's biggest fool, Malone," said he, "not to take a steady job and settle down with that little girl. Nowhere in the world will you find her equal as a cook."

"Nor would I find a girl to match Nellie in any other respect," Barney agreed. "But not even for Nellie would I make myself a prisoner in a factory or a shop. And if I did I'd be doing her a wrong, for I'd end up by driving her as mad as the job would drive me."

It was then that inspiration came to Mr. Hennessy. "I wonder," he said, "would there be any truth in the saying that you've to set a thief to catch a thief? How would you like to be water bailiff when Sam Wheeler retires next month?"

"It's the only steady job in the world that I'd want to take," Barney answered.

"But, mind you, if I recommend you, you mustn't let me down," Mr. Hennessy warned him. "There must be no more poaching."

"I'll see to that, Mr. Hennessy," said Nellie from the doorway, and there was a light in her eye which told both men that Barney's poaching days were ended.

Baked Boyne River Salmon

Ingredients: 4 pounds fresh salmon, 1 medium onion, 4 tablespoons butter, 2 lemons, salt and pepper.

Method: Portion the salmon into six generous steaks. Rub with lemon and brush generously with butter. Sprinkle lightly with salt and pepper. Place in buttered pan and bake 20 minutes in a moderate (375°) oven.

This dish is at its most toothsome best when accompanied by a salad of sliced cucumber and onion marinated in French dressing and a dish of mealy potatoes boiled in their jackets. Serve with Emerald Sauce made as follows:

Emerald Sauce

Melt 4 tablespoons butter over moderate heat. Blend in 4 tablespoons flour and stir, without browning, until a dry paste is formed. Add, stirring constantly, 2 cups boiled milk. Simmer gently, stirring occasionally, 15 minutes. Now add 1 cup spinach purée. Simmer 5 minutes and remove from heat. Stir in 2 egg yolks blended with ½ cup cream. Reheat, without boiling, and season to taste. Serve the salmon on a platter coated with the luscious green sauce and garnished with lemon wedges and parsley sprigs.

Craibheacháin of Sea Food

Pronounced "crave-a-hawn" this long word can mean any minced, savory mixture. In an early Irish translation of the Bible we are told that "Esau sold his birthright for a craibheacháin."

Ingredients: 1 cup each cooked lobster, shrimp, salmon, crabmeat, and codfish; 1 clove garlic, crushed; 2 medium onions, chopped; 2 leeks, chopped; 1 head lettuce, 2 lemons, 6 sprigs parsley, dash tabasco, 6 radishes, 4 tablespoons butter, pepper and salt to taste.

Method: Sauté in butter until tender (but without browning) the chopped onions, leeks, and garlic. Pass through a fine food chopper together with lobster, shrimp, salmon, crabmeat, and codfish. Season with salt, pepper, and tabasco and let cool. Place a mound of the mixture on a cup-shaped leaf of lettuce in individual dishes. Garnish with a lemon wedge, a sprig of parsley, and a radish rose. Serve with any zesty cocktail sauce.

Dingle Mackerel

Ingredients: 6 small mackerel, 2 cups vinegar, 1 bay leaf, 2 teaspoons salt, few grains cayenne, 6 peppercorns, 3 sprigs parsley, 1-inch stick cinnamon.

Method: Cut off heads and fins. Wash and clean mackerel, split, and remove backbones and tails. Roll up and place in a deep pie dish. Add spices, bay leaf, parsley, and seasoning. Add vinegar. Cover and simmer 45 minutes in a 375° oven.

Donegal Lobster

Plunge lobster into boiling water and boil 5 minutes. Drain and cool. Remove claws. With a sharp knife split lobster from head to tail and right through tail. Remove black vein, small sac at back of head, and spongy material. Crack claws gently with a hammer. With a sharp knife make 2 crosscuts in tail to prevent curling. Brush with melted butter and broil 5 minutes under moderate heat. Turn, brush with butter, and broil other side 5 minutes. Serve with melted butter and lemon wedges. Return to lobster shell any meat that may have fallen into broiler during cooking and pour the butter from the pan over the cooked lobster.

Dublin Bay Cocktail

Ingredients: 2 pounds jumbo shrimp, 1 head lettuce, 1 cup mayonnaise, 2 lemons, beet juice, dash tabasco, salt and pepper to taste, parsley.

Method: Remove veins and drop shrimp into boiling water for 6-8 minutes. Leave until cool. In an individual dish place 5 shrimp on a cup-shaped leaf of lettuce. Season the mayonnaise with the juice of 1 lemon, tabasco, salt and pepper, and thin to desired consistency with beet juice. Top the shrimp with the sauce. Serve cold with a wedge of lemon and a sprig of parsley.

Dublin Cockles (Scalloped)

Allow 1 pint (about ¾ pound) cockles per person.

Ingredients: 4 pints (3 pounds) cockles, 4 tablespoons butter, 1¼ cups fine breadcrumbs, 2 teaspoons salt, ½ teaspoon pepper, ½ cup cider or white wine.

Method: Wash the cockles well and leave 1 hour in slightly salted water. Drain, place in pan without adding extra water. Add cider or white wine. Cover closely and cook about 5 minutes over moderate heat (shaking the pan frequently) until the shells open. Remove from shells, set aside, and reserve liquor. Place a layer of seasoned breadcrumbs in a large fire-proof dish or in individual dishes. Place the cockles on top. Cover with breadcrumbs, moisten with the cockle liquor, dot with butter, and bake 10 minutes in a hot (450°) oven.

Eel Pratie Manglam

("Pratie" is the affectionate country name for potatoes. "Manglam" is one of the Irish words for pie.)

Ingredients: 2 pounds (6 medium) potatoes, 2 pounds eels, 2 table-spoons bacon fat, 1 tablespoon chopped parsley, 2 teaspoons salt, 1 tea-spoon pepper, 1 tablespoon flour, 2 tablespoons chopped onion, 2 table-spoons butter, ½ cup cider, ½ cup cream, 1 egg.

Method: Boil the potatoes in their jackets, peel and mash well, season with half of the pepper and salt; add butter and cream and beat until light and fluffy. (Potatoes mashed in this way are called "poundies.") Line the sides of a pie dish with poundies, reserving enough for a topping. Mix the flour with remaining pepper and salt. Skin and clean the eels and cut in 2-inch pieces. Melt the bacon fat in a pan over quick heat. Brown the eels on all sides and place in the pie dish. Now fry the onions in the same fat until light brown. Add parsley and cider to the onions and pour over the eels. Top with poundies. Ruffle the top with a fork, brush with beaten egg, and bake 50 minutes in a 400° oven. When done, make a hole in the center and pour in a sauce made as follows:

Combine 2 tablespoons white stock with ½ cup cream and bring to a boil. Knead 1 tablespoon flour with 1 tablespoon butter and add to the cream mixture. Simmer 3 minutes and season with salt and pepper, a pinch of nutmeg, and a teaspoon of lemon juice.

N.B.: A handful of chopped oysters added to the pie instead of the parsley lifts this good dish into the *haute cuisine* class.

Herrings (Potted)

Ingredients: 6 herrings, 3 peppercorns, ½ cup white vinegar, ½ cup water, ½ teaspoon ground mace, 1 bay leaf, 4 cloves, 1 teaspoon salt, ½ teaspoon pepper.

Method: Clean and dry herrings. Cut off heads, tails, and fins, and split the fish from head to tail. Remove backbones. Sprinkle with salt and pepper, roll up, place in pie dish. Add peppercorns, cloves, mace, bay leaf, water, and vinegar. Cover and bake 50 minutes at 375°.

Liffey Trout (with Mushroom Sauce)

I have known the delight of preparing and eating this dish after catching the trout myself in a leaf-dappled stretch of the Liffey. And, on the way home, I stopped at a field where "cuppeens" (little button mushrooms) nestled like fallen stars among the tufts of grass. There are few joys on earth to compare with gathering mushrooms in the early morning. Next best is to buy your trout and your mushrooms and to prepare the fish in this way:

Ingredients: 4 small trout, ½ cup (¼ pound) butter, ½ cup flour, 1 cup of half cream and half milk, 1 tablespoon chopped parsley, about 12 button mushrooms, pepper and salt.

Method: Clean, wash, and dry the trout. Roll in ¼ cup of the flour seasoned with pepper and salt. Fry in ¼ cup of the butter. Drain and keep hot. Wipe and slice the mushrooms and sauté in the fat in which the trout were fried. Melt remaining butter in a small saucepan, stir in flour. Add milk and cream and season to taste. Add mushrooms and reheat to serving point. Garnish the trout with parsley and serve sauce separately.

Lough Neagh Eel Stew

According to Thomas Moore:

> On Lough Neagh's banks where the fisherman strays
> Ere the clear cold eve's declining,
> He sees the round towers of other days
> In the waves beneath him shining.

He also sees—if he's lucky—a species of conger eel which makes a lip-smacking casserole. When, during the war, I found myself in Belfast where everything except fish was in short supply, I bought 1½ pounds of sturdy, milky Lough Neagh eels. Using whatever ingredients were available, I made them into a casserole which the family loved. A few months ago I was given a copy of Jean Conil's *Gastronomic Tour de France*. In the section on Basses-Alpes specialties I found a recipe for an eel casserole which was almost a replica of the eel recipe I had imagined was my own exclusive creation. It just goes to show that there's telepathy among cooks.

Ingredients: ¼ cup butter (the French use oil), 1 medium onion, 1½ pounds skinned and sliced eel, 1 medium carrot, a bouquet garni, 2 cups cider (in France they use white wine), salt and pepper to taste, 2 large tomatoes, 1 clove garlic, 4 large potatoes.

Method: Heat the butter in a pan over moderate heat. Add the chopped onion and cook gently until golden. Add the skinned eel, cut in 1½-inch slices. Cover with cider. Add the sliced carrot, and bouquet garni. Season with salt and pepper. Cover and cook 20 minutes. Remove the eel slices. Add to the cooking liquor the skinned and sliced tomatoes, crushed garlic, and pared and quartered potatoes. Cover and cook until the potatoes are tender. Add the eel slices and reheat. In the Basses-Alpes they like to add a pinch of saffron. Personally I think the eel stew looks and tastes better without it.

The second and most tragic of what are known as "The Three Sorrows of Irish Story-Telling" concerns the four children of King Lir who lived in pre-Christian times. When Lir became a widower he married a beautiful woman called Eva.

For a while Eva doted on her three stepsons and on her beautiful stepdaughter, Fionnuala. But when she found that her husband's heart was set on his children her love for them turned to bitter jealousy and hatred.

According to the old legend a devil got into her when she awoke one night to find that Lir was missing from their bed and, going in search of him, she discovered him gazing fondly at the faces of his sleeping children.

In her youth Eva had learned something of witchcraft. Now she remembered a wicked spell she had seen practiced and she determined to use it to make Lir her own.

One day she took the children to Lake Derravaragh near Mullingar. "Get into the water and wash away the dust of the journey," she told them. While the children were splashing about in the sandy shallows, Eva struck them with a wand. At once the children were changed into four snowy swans.

Eva was frightened by what she had done, but she could not undo the spell. But she was able to mitigate her wickedness just a little. "In nine hundred years' time, when the first Mass bell will ring in Ireland, your human shape will be returned to you," she told them.

(The first three hundred years were to be spent by the unfortunate four on Lake Derravaragh, the second three hundred years on the Sea of Noyle, and the final three hundred years in the gray seas off Mayo's bleak Erris Point.)

Eva did not profit as she had hoped by her wickedness. King Lir cast her off and came to live on the shores of Derravaragh where he stayed close to his swan-children until he died.

The story of how Fionnuala looked after her brothers during those nine hundred years deserves Walt Disney's genius.

At long last the day came when they heard the Mass bell of Saint Keevog. The four swans winged their way to the Saint's little church where they were baptized. It is said that immediately after their baptism, their feathers fell from them and they reverted to human form, but incredibly aged and wrinkled. And no sooner had the Saint given them the Last Sacrament than their souls left their tired bodies and flew straight to Heaven.

And this story of the children of Lir explains why swan, which was considered royal food elsewhere, is never mentioned in accounts of ancient Irish banquets. Until this day to kill a swan is an unforgivable sin in Ireland.

From poetry to pike is not such a long step, particularly when the pike is from Lake Derravaragh and is made into a poem of a dish in this way:

Pike Derravaragh

Ingredients: 1 pike (about 3 pounds), 1 cup poultry dressing, ¼ pound streaky bacon, 4 tablespoons butter, ½ cup sherry, pepper and salt.

Method: Clean, trim, and scale fish. Wipe well, season the cavity with pepper and salt and fill loosely with dressing. Sew or skewer together. Place in a greased baking tin. Cover with streaky bacon and place in a 375° oven. Bake 50 minutes, basting frequently with sherry and melted butter. Serve with tartare sauce.

Poached Salmon (with Buttered Leeks and Potatoes)

Ingredients: 2 pounds fresh salmon, 12 leeks, 1 cup (½ pound) butter,

2 pounds (6 medium) potatoes, ½ cup cider vinegar, ½ teaspoon all-spice, 1 teaspoon salt, minced parsley.

Method: Portion the salmon into six steaks. Place in a shallow pan with the allspice, vinegar, and salt. Cover with water and poach for 20 minutes. Pare and boil the potatoes. Dot them with butter and sprinkle with parsley. Split the leeks, wash and boil them. Serve each poached salmon steak on a platter with potatoes at one end and the leeks at the other. Cover with drawn butter and top with a sprig of parsley.

Wexford Sole (in Cider Sauce)

Ingredients: 1½ pounds sole filets, a pinch of paprika, ½ cup cider, 4 tablespoons butter, 3 tablespoons flour, ½ cup cream, about 6 medium mushrooms, salt and pepper, 1 tablespoon chopped parsley.

Method: Place fish in a shallow, greased baking pan. If the filets are large, cut them in half. Sprinkle with paprika. Pour cider over them. Bake the fish in a moderate (375°) oven until just tender, basting now and then with the cider. When tender remove the filets carefully to a hot fireproof dish and keep hot while you make the sauce as follows: Melt butter in a saucepan. Stir in flour. Add gradually the liquid in which the fish was baked, and stir and cook until the sauce is smooth and boiling. Reduce the heat, stir in salt and pepper to taste, and add cream.

Stir over very low heat until the sauce is hot, but do not allow to boil. Add sliced mushrooms blanched in boiling water. Pour the sauce over the filets. Place them under the grill for a few minutes until the sauce is bubbly and lightly browned in spots.

6

Vegetables

"It is better to be invited to herbs with love, than to a fatted calf with hatred."

Proverbs XV, 17

*T*he way Lottie Fenlon hated onions was a great hardship on Hugh Doherty.

"Miss Fenlon has agreed to take you as a boarder," Father Molloy told Hugh when he first came to Ballyderrig to oversee the renovation of the church. "She's a grand cook. You'll be comfortable with her."

At fifty, good cooking and comfort were very important to Hugh.

Lottie bore out the priest's recommendation. In return for his two pounds ten shillings a week her boarder got a good fire, a good bed, a comfortable armchair, and the pleasant companionship of his gentle-voiced landlady. Her soda bread was feather-like, her roasts dripped juice, and she had a way with sauces that could transform the most pallid bit of boiled cod into a fast-day feast.

For Hugh her cooking had one big lack. She never used onions. Hugh was partial to onions. He liked them fried as his mother used to cook them. Not the grease-sodden discolored strings which so many women pass off as fried onions, but those crisp, golden-brown rings, tender and succulent, which you get if the rings are separated, tossed in seasoned flour, dipped in batter, and then fried for 3 minutes in boiling fat.

There were few dishes he liked more than boiled onions smothered in cheese sauce, topped with breadcrumbs, and browned in the oven. He adored baby onions chopped small and added with hot milk and a lump of butter to fluffy mashed potatoes. Given his choice of supper-time sandwiches, he would swear that there was nothing to beat buttered whole-meal bread and thin slivers of Spanish onion, well seasoned.

But Lottie would not let an onion into the house. The reason was psychological. Onions had been responsible for the wrecking of her first and only romance. It had happened twenty years before when she was seventeen and in love with a bank clerk, called Cecil Quin, a very refined young man who would have died rather than be seen in the street without his yellow gloves and his walking stick.

Lottie's romance crashed the evening she had onions for tea before meeting Cecil for their bi-weekly walk along the canal bank. If Mrs. Fenlon had lived long enough to tell her daughter the facts of life Lottie would have known that, provided proper precautions are taken, a girl may eat an acre of onions without fear of alienating her boy-friend, however refined. She would have been taught that a glass of milk sipped slowly or a mouthful of parsley chewed leisurely will destroy all evidence of onion-eating.

But poor Lottie was an uninstructed orphan. When, on that fateful evening, Cecil bent to give her one of his carefully rationed kisses, she was hurt and dismayed to see him rear back offendedly. He left her with a quick good night and never took her out again. A year later he married Angela Murphy, who was as refined as himself and who had a good dowry into the bargain. To complete Lottie's humiliation, Angela told all Ballyderrig of the solecism which had killed the bank clerk's love. From that day Lottie turned her back on men and onions.

After Hugh came to board with her, he made a few tentative suggestions regarding the culinary uses of onions . . . that though steak was good with mushrooms, it was even better with onion rings . . . that poultry dressing was not the same, somehow, without onions.

Lottie freezed him. "If you want onions, Mr. Doherty," she said, her voice trembling, "I'm afraid you will have to find accommodation elsewhere. Inside this door an onion will never come!"

After that he put up with the lack of his favorite vegetable, feeling that Lottie's house afforded compensations which atoned. She was glad he stayed. Since his coming she had discovered that a woman who lives alone can be very lonely.

When he had been with her about three months Lottie had to go to Dublin to see about a tooth that was worrying her. "I won't be able to get a bus back until the morning," she told him. "If I leave you to look after yourself for the night, will you be all right?"

Hugh assured her that he could manage. Just the same, she was worried. Therefore, when she walked into Father Molloy in Dublin that evening she was glad to accept his offer of a lift home.

As she stepped into her beeswaxed hall she stopped dead and sniffed. There was no mistaking the smell. Onions were being cooked in her kitchen!

She threw open the kitchen door. There was Mr. Doherty, one of her aprons tied around his ample middle, happily engaged in basting something that sent its aroma through the house. At her step he turned quickly and dropped the spoon. Guilt and dismay made his flushed face several shades redder.

"I'm—I'm sorry!" he stammered, hanging his head. "I—I was making stuffed onions the way my mother used to do them."

There was something in the big man's apologetic humility, in the disarray of his wispy fair hair, and in his scared blue eyes which awoke the latent maternalism in Lottie Fenlon. All at once the anger left her. The bitterness of years went from her. It was replaced by something soft and warm which made her look ten years younger.

Hugh Doherty saw the transformation. In some peculiar way it made him stop feeling like a schoolboy caught stealing apples. Instead, he felt like a masterful man. He acted like one, too. In two strides he was across the kitchen and had Lottie in his arms.

For their betrothal supper they ate the stuffed onions. Luckily, Hugh had cooked enough for two.

Let me be honest. We Irish are not too strong on vegetables. Artichokes, asparagus, avocados, aubergines, and suchlike: these are not everyday fare with us.

Our vegetables, for the most part, are limited to potatoes, cabbage, cauliflower, onions, beans, peas, turnips, parsnips, celery, beets, lettuce, and watercress. We have herbs in plenty, but few of us take advantage of them.

Potatoes, of course, have been our first choice ever since Sir Walter Raleigh brought them with tobacco from Virginia and planted them in his garden at Youghal, County Cork. Incidentally, we have to thank Raleigh, too, for cherries and wallflowers. His house at Youghal still stands, and the descendents of the first Irish-grown wallflowers still run riot there.

There was a time when new potatoes were not available until June 29, the Feast of Sts. Peter and Paul. But in recent years the Brandon (Kerry) Co-operative Farmers' Association has been able to supply city restaurants with new potatoes from the sheltered slopes of Brandon as early as St. Patrick's Day. (There was a tradition among the early Irish that Brandon was the original Garden of Eden.)

Brandon Parslied Potatoes

Wash Brandon early potatoes under running water and rub the tender skins from them with a vegetable brush. Put them to cook in boiling salted water containing a leaf or two of mint. When cooked (they'll take only about 10 minutes) drain well, remove mint, and toss potatoes gently over moderate heat to dry them. Add a good knob of butter. When the potatoes are evenly coated with butter turn them into a hot dish and sprinkle liberally with finely chopped parsley.

Cabbage (Braised)

Ingredients: 1 medium Savoy cabbage, 4 tablespoons chopped onion, 2 tablespoons butter; 2 large tomatoes, skinned, seeded, and chopped; 1 tablespoon flour, 1 cup white stock, 4 tablespoons sour cream, 2 teaspoons finely chopped parsley, pepper and salt to taste.

Method: Quarter cabbage, remove most of stalk, cover with boiling water, and leave to blanch 10 minutes. Drain and pat dry in a towel. Place in a glass oven dish. Melt butter over moderate heat and sauté onions until tender but not brown. Remove onions with a slotted spoon and arrange over cabbage. Put chopped tomatoes in fat, stir in flour, add stock, and bring to a boil, stirring constantly. Add seasoning and parsley, mix well, and spoon the mixture over the quartered cabbage. Cook covered in a moderate (375°) oven about 45 minutes, basting occasionally. Fifteen minutes before cabbage is done, add the sour cream.

When all is said and done, I doubt if any cabbage dish will ever wean us Irish from our liking for greasy cabbage—a good bolster of it—on which reclines a piece of boiled bacon or ham.

Slieve na mBan Carrots

The ruddy crest of Slieve na mBan (The Mountain of the Women) rising above its stole of milk-white mist gives its name to this dish of cream-wreathed carrots.

Ingredients: 12 young carrots, 3 tablespoons butter, ½ cup milk, ½ cup cream, yolks of 2 eggs, 1 teaspoon finely chopped parsley, pepper and salt to taste.

Method: Trim and wash carrots and halve lengthwise. Melt butter over moderate heat, add milk, season with salt and pepper, add carrots, and cook gently until tender. Remove from heat, stir in cream and beaten egg yolks, and reheat but do not boil, stirring until eggs thicken. Correct seasoning and add parsley.

Cauliflower Souse

Cook a large cauliflower in boiling salted water. Drain and break or cut into about 8 pieces. Season well, drench in black butter (butter which has been heated until *light brown* in a frying pan). Top with toasted bread-crumbs.

Colcannon

This delectable mixture of buttered greens and potatoes is yet another way of foretelling the future at Halloween. A heaped portion is served on each plate. A well is made in the center of the heap to hold a generous lump of butter. The colcannon is eaten from around the outside of the heap, each person dipping his fork first into the colcannon and then into the melting butter. The perfect accompaniment to colcannon is a glass of fresh buttermilk.

> Did you ever eat colcannon when 'twas made with yellow cream,
> And the kale and praties blended like the picture in a dream?
> Did you ever take a forkful and dip it in the lake
> Of the clover-flavored butter that your mother used to make?
> Did you ever eat and eat, afraid you'd let the ring go past,
> And some old married sour-puss would get it at the last?
> Oh, you did; yes, you did. So did he and so did I,
> And the more I think about it, sure the more I want to cry.
> Ah, God be with the happy times when troubles we had not,
> And our mothers made colcannon in the little three-legged pot.

To the old song's nostalgic questionnaire I would add: Did you ever know the thrill of believing you had found that lucky ring or silver coin in your portion of one of our national Halloween dishes? And were you ever cruelly disappointed when what you hoped was a paper-wrapped coin turned out to be merely a lump of hard potato?

The prevention of such heartache is a simple matter. Here is a recipe for perfect colcannon. Put the cooked potatoes through a sieve or ricer. Beat in a good lump of butter and enough hot cream or milk to make the mixture light and fluffy. Add to the potato mixture one-half its bulk of finely chopped cooked kale and a tablespoon of minced onion. Add pepper and salt to taste, beat well, and reheat thoroughly. And don't forget the ring and that all-important silver coin.

In the Midlands colcannon is called "Thump." In the North and West it is called "Champ." Up North the children have a rhyme to which they skip. It goes:

> There was an old woman who lived in a lamp
> And she had no room to beetle her champ
> So she up with her beetle and broke the lamp,
> And then she had room to beetle her champ.

Dulce Champ

Dulce is an edible seaweed which some Irish chew as Americans chew gum. It is at its best in August. At the Auld Lammas (Lambs') Fair in Ballycastle there are always stalls of dulce and of Yalla Man—a kind of toffee. This custom has inspired the song:

> At the Auld Lammas Fair in Ballycastle O
> Were you ever at the fair in Ballycastle O?
> Did you treat your Mary Anne
> To dulce and Yalla Man
> At the Auld Lammas Fair in Ballycastle O

To make dulce champ soak fresh dulce in cold water 3 hours. Drain and simmer until tender in milk to cover. Drain and chop fine. Combine with an equal quantity of mashed potatoes, a good lump of butter, and sufficient of the milk in which the dulce was cooked to make the champ light. Season to taste and beat until fluffy.

Haggerty

Ingredients: 3 medium potatoes, 1 large onion, ¾ cup grated cheddar cheese, 2 tablespoons bacon fat, pepper and salt to taste.

Method: Wash and pare potatoes, cut in paper-thin slices and pat dry in a towel. Slice onions very thin. Heat half the bacon fat in a heavy frying pan, alternate layers of potatoes and onions and a sprinkling of pepper and salt, finishing with potatoes. Dot the top layer of potatoes with remainder of bacon fat. Cook over moderate heat until potatoes are almost tender.

Turn the haggerty carefully onto a platter, slip it, topside down, back into the pan and continue cooking until done. To serve, cut in wedges.

Leekie Manglam

Leeks have always occupied a favored place in Irish cooking—and with good reason. Their popularity dates back to the days of St. Patrick. One day, so the story goes, a chieftain who was being driven out of his mind by his pregnant wife's demands for leeks (then out of season), implored the saint's help. St. Patrick took a few juicy rushes, blessed them, and turned them into leeks which immediately cured the unfortunate woman's "longing sickness" and brought peace to her harassed husband. There and then St. Patrick ordained that any woman suffering from the "longing sickness" (modern doctors call it "pica" or "morbid craving") should be cured if she ate any member of the onion family.

Leekie Manglam (leek pasty) is well worth trying, even if one is not in an interesting condition.

Ingredients: ⅓ recipe for Lardy Cakes (p. 37), 3 large leeks, 4 slices streaky bacon, ½ cup breadcrumbs, ¼ cup milk, pepper and salt to taste, 1 egg.

Method: Parboil the leeks, drain, and cut them into very thin slices, add the diced bacon, mix in crumbs, milk, and seasoning. Divide the pastry in two. Use half to line a pie plate. Fill with the leek mixture. Brush edges with water. Cover with a lid of pastry. Press edges firmly together and flute. Brush with beaten egg and bake 30 minutes in a 425° oven.

Nettle Briseach

Briseach (pronounced brishock) is any food which is cooked to a pulp—in other words, a purée. Not so long ago, if you strayed along a country road in springtime you would find women gathering nettles, their hands and arms protected by black woolen stockings. Although few of us wear such stockings nowadays outside convents, many women find young nettles a handy stand-by while they are waiting for the spring cabbage to be ready for pulling. And gloves are just as good a protection from nettle stings as were those hand-knitted stockings.

Ingredients: 3 pounds nettles, 2 tablespoons butter, 2 tablespoons flour, pepper and salt.

Method: Pick the leaves from the stalks and wash well in several lots of cold water. Put into a saucepan with a sprinkling of salt and barely enough water to keep from burning. Cook uncovered about 15 minutes, occasionally pressing down the nettles and turning them over with a wooden spoon. When tender, drain well, chop fine (or rub through a sieve). Melt the butter over moderate heat, add the nettles, stir in the flour, season well with pepper and add more salt if needed. Stir over moderate heat 5-6 minutes.

Nettles are good eaten à la spinach with poached eggs. In Ireland we prefer to eat this wholesome vegetable with fried or boiled bacon or ham.

Pease Pudding

Ingredients: ½ pound dried peas, 2 tablespoons butter, 1 egg, 1 teaspoon salt, ½ teaspoon pepper, 2 teaspoons sugar.

Method: Wash and pick over peas; soak overnight in cold water. Tie loosely in muslin, leaving plenty of room for the peas to swell. Simmer until tender in water containing ½ teaspoon salt and 1 teaspoon sugar. Rub through a sieve, add pepper and ½ teaspoon salt, butter, and beaten egg. Place in a greased pie dish, cover, and bake 30 minutes in a moderate (375°) oven.

Potato Collops

There is no denying that the best way of all to cook potatoes is to boil or bake them in their jackets. And, notwithstanding the advice of foreign cooks, the skins of potatoes to be boiled should not be gashed when being put to cook. If the skins should burst slightly in the boiling and subsequent drying (boiled potatoes should always be shaken for a minute or two over low heat after being drained) it is all to the good: there is no more appetizing sight than the floury "grin" of a burst boiled potato.

Admittedly, during the weeks before the new potatoes are ready for digging, last season's potatoes begin to show their age and sometimes need dressing up. And I know of few better potato dishes than Collops ("collop," by the way, means a small portion of any foodstuff). Originally "collope," the sixteenth-century Irish referred to our famous rashers and eggs as "collopes and eggs."

Ingredients: 3 medium potatoes, 1 large onion, ¼ pound diced raw bacon (to be omitted on fast days), 2 teaspoons chopped parsley, pepper and salt to taste, 1 cup boiled milk, 2 tablespoons butter, 3 tablespoons grated cheese.

Method: Pare potatoes and cut into very thin slices. Chop onion. Place a layer of vegetables in a greased baking dish. Sprinkle with seasonings and diced bacon (rind removed) and dot with butter. Repeat layers until all ingredients are used, finishing with potatoes. Pour in milk and sprinkle top with grated cheese. Cover and bake 45 minutes in a moderate (350°) oven. Uncover and continue cooking until potatoes are done and top layer is brown.

Potato Scrapple

Mix equal quantities of cooked greens and poundies (potatoes mashed with butter and milk or cream). Season well. Add enough milk to make the mixture moist, but not wet. Heat some bacon dripping very hot in the frying pan, turn the potato mixture onto it, spread evenly, and fry until brown. Turn it, cutting it roughly with the knife as it cooks, the idea being to make the finished result an appetizing collection of crisp brown pieces.

Any cooked greens are good in this dish—sprouts, kale, spinach, etc.

SALADS

Our Irish salads may not be so varied as those in other parts of the world, but there is evidence that long before the people of other countries got wise to the valuable properties of raw vegetables, we in Ireland made them a part of our daily diet.

St. Patrick's favorite herb was garlic. His cook, Aithchen (who is, incidentally, the patron saint of Irish cooks), made sure that he had a plentiful supply of this most powerful of interior disinfectants when accompanying Patrick on his travels through Ireland. St. Ciaran found that he could live comfortably on a daily diet of carrot salad and barley bread. Over a thousand years ago a certain Bishop Erc of Slane liked to treat himself occasionally to a hard-cooked goose egg accompanied by a salad of watercress. And sorrel, with its delicate sourness, was a favorite ingredient of our salads which, with the advent of the English, changed their name to "sallets." Today, Dublin's street vendors still use this Elizabethan word for lettuce. In Moore Street you'll hear them cry, "Lovely sallet, thruppence a head."

Nowadays we serve all the salads eaten elsewhere, but Slane salad continues to be a favorite amalgam of good food and old memories.

Ingredients: 1 pound sorrel leaves, 3 tart apples, 2 cups watercress leaves, 2 young carrots, French dressing.

Method: Pare the apples, core, and slice thin. Clean carrots and cut in julienne strips. Place the sorrel and watercress in a bowl and cover with apple slices. Sprinkle carrots on top. Serve with a French dressing to which a garlic flavor has been given in this way: impale a clove of garlic on the fork with which you beat the dressing.

7

❋ Meat, Poultry, Game ❋

"...they took their meat with gladness and with simplicity of heart ..."
Acts XI, 46

*O*n a bleak day even to think of Statia Dunne's stew brings comfort. That was a monarch among stews. It won Statia many a compliment. It won her a husband—and that at an age when she had almost given up hope of ever having a man of her own to cook for.

Statia was not the type to catch a man's eye. She had pale hair and skin, and she was small and shy. Given a little leisure she might have done something with herself, but caring for her bedridden father and for her three bachelor brothers left her with barely enough time to bless herself.

She was nearing forty when Dr. Crowley came to our place. He was at the age when a man who is not married begins to show the need of a woman who'll see that his clothes are pressed and his collars properly laundered, and who'll make sure that he eats good regular meals. Poor Dr. Crowley looked lost and neglected.

He was called out to old Mr. Dunne during that spell of cold, stormy weather we had five—or was it six?—years ago.

The house was filled with the smell of Statia's stew. It was a tantalizing smell, made up of twenty different fragrances. As Dr. Crowley was drawing on his gloves, he nodded in the direction of the kitchen. "That's a grand smell," he said shyly.

Statia said afterward that he looked like a child putting in for a treat. The lost look of him coupled with the way the sleet was pelting the windows made her say quickly, "Wouldn't you stay and have a bit? I was just putting it on the table."

Dr. Crowley found the look of the stew even more tantalizing than the smell. Statia believed in serving a good dish in the style it deserved. Around the edge of a big platter she built a rampart of fluffy mashed potato. That was given a quick brown-up in the oven, after which she bedewed it with parsley, chopped powder-fine. The stew was turned into this gold and jade ring. Brown of tender meat cubes mingled with the white of celery and turnip, the bright green of peas, and the yellow and orange of carrots, the whole soused in gravy as dark and as rich as a maharajah.

That gravy was the making of Statia's stew. Years of practice had gone to finding out the exact amount of mustard that should be added for tanginess, of sugar for the faint underlying sweetness, and of vinegar for a teasing sharpness. It had a leaf of this herb, a sprig of that. And it was full of the goodness of the meat and vegetable juices which had run into it during the slow careful cooking.

Dr. Crowley cleared his plate. As he stood up to go Statia could not help thinking that if only his clothes were pressed once in a while he could look as prosperous and as comfortable as any doctor in Ireland.

"Do you know," he said, "I haven't eaten a meal like that since my mother died, God rest her."

"We have stew every Saturday during the cold weather," Statia told him. "You'd be very welcome any time you'd be passing."

In the way one thing leads to another Dr. Crowley got acquainted with Statia's stuffed steak, her coddled rabbit, and her baked liver loaf served with scalloped potatoes. Before he was halfway through her culinary repertoire they were engaged.

She took old Mr. Dunne to live with them when they got married. And her eldest brother, Paddy, who had been keeping company with Leesha Flood for sixteen years, married the girl and brought her home to take Statia's place. So that she might do this adequately Statia bought a twopenny copybook and wrote out the best of her recipes for her sister-in-law. Leesha let me copy them and I have them to thank for the fact that I'm a happy married woman today. But that's another story.

By the way, Statia's trick of serving the stew in a ring of toasted mashed potato was one she often employed when she wanted to dress up creamed vegetables or fish or leftover meat heated in gravy.

There was a time when, in common with the rest of the no-refrigerator world, we made liberal use of spices to disguise meat that was "high." Nowadays we use spice to enhance the flavor of the cheaper cuts of meat—particularly beef and mutton. The meat is placed in a deep dish, soused with a cider marinade, and left for a few hours.

Cider Marinade

Combine 1½ cups cider, 2 small sliced onions, ½ teaspoon ginger, 3 whole cloves, ½ teaspoon cinnamon, 3 tablespoons sugar. Strained, the marinade makes a good base for sauce or gravy to serve with the meat.

Baked Limerick Ham

Long ago a whole pig would have been baked in a pit lined with stones previously heated in the fire. Or it might have been cooked in one of the great bronze cauldrons which were the most treasured possessions of well-to-do households. Pork was always the favorite meat of the Irish. (Wasn't it as a swineherd that St. Patrick first came to us?) When the meat was cooked the various cuts were served according to the social importance of the guests:

A thigh for a king and a poet;
A chine for a literary sage;
A leg for a young lord;
Heads for charioteers;
A haunch for a queen.

"The hero's morsel" was the choice tidbit reserved for the man who had performed the greatest or bravest exploit ... and woe betide anyone who helped himself to it if he was not entitled to the honor. One of the biggest battles in Irish history occurred because a chieftain wrongfully appropriated "the hero's morsel."

Ingredients: 1 10-pound Limerick ham, 2 teaspoons whole cloves, 1 cup Madeira wine, ¾ cup honey.

Method: Soak the ham in cold water for 12 hours. Place in a pot, cover well with fresh water, and bring slowly to a boil. Allow to simmer for 2 hours. Place the ham in a baking pan, remove the skin, and stick cloves over the entire surface. Pour the honey mixed with Madeira wine over the ham and bake in a moderate (350°) oven for 2½ hours until the knuckle bone can be removed. Serve with the following sauce:

Antrim Sauce

Ingredients: 1 onion, 1 cup flour, 1 tablespoon tomato paste, 2 cups stock or water, 1 cup (½ pound) butter, 1 cup Madeira wine, 1 tablespoon dry mustard, salt and pepper to taste, 1 teaspoon sugar.

Method: Chop the onion fine and sauté in butter. Mix in the flour and stir until golden brown. Mix in the stock or water and cook for 20 minutes. Add mustard, tomato paste, Madeira wine, and sugar, and boil for another 10 minutes. Season to taste with salt and pepper.

Beef Pot Roast (Seventeenth-Century)

Ingredients: 3 pounds beef (select a thick solid piece), 1 cup veal forcemeat, 4 slices fat bacon, 1½ cups water or stock, 1 cup red wine, 2 tablespoons flour, 3 tablespoons beef dripping, pepper and salt, 4 medium mushrooms.

Method: Make holes here and there in the beef and fill with forcemeat.

Lay the strips of bacon on top and tie in place. Mix pepper and salt with flour, rub into the meat, and sear it quickly on all sides in smoking hot dripping. Place in a heavy pan, add water, wine, and a sprinkling of salt and pepper. Cover and simmer until tender. When done, place meat on a platter, remove bacon and string and keep the meat hot. Skim fat from the liquor, add the sliced mushrooms, thicken with a tablespoon of butter kneaded with a tablespoon of flour, bring to a boil, and simmer 5 minutes. Serve the gravy separately. This beef is excellent cold.

Bog of Allen Game Pie

Ingredients: Brace of grouse or 1 pheasant, 2 young rabbits ("coneens" we call them), ¼ pound fat bacon, 1 carrot, 1 onion, 1 stalk celery, 2 tablespoons butter, ½ teaspoon anchovy paste, ¼ cup port wine, ½ cup giblet stock, salt and pepper to taste, 2 tablespoons flour, ⅛ recipe Puff Pastry (p. 46), 1 egg.

Method: Cut cleaned grouse or partridge into neat pieces. Cut each prepared rabbit in pieces. Dice vegetables. Mix flour with seasoning and coat game and rabbits. Remove rind from bacon, dice and brown quickly in a heavy pan. Add prepared vegetables, stock, and wine. Cover and simmer until meat is tender. Transfer meat to pie dish. Strain cooking liquor and add anchovy paste. Pour over meat and top with thin pastry. Crimp edges, decorate with a pastry rose on top, making a hole in center to allow steam to escape. Brush with beaten egg. Bake 20-25 minutes in a hot (450°) oven.

Brawn

Ingredients: 1 pig's head (unsalted), 1 tablespoon salt, ½ cup cider, 2 bay leaves, 2 teaspoons peppercorns, 6 cloves.

Method: Prepare the pig's head as for boiling. Cut in 4 pieces. Put all ingredients in a heavy saucepan and add sufficient cold water barely to cover. Simmer 2 hours, or until the flesh falls away from the bones. Strain off the liquor into another saucepan and boil it rapidly, uncovered, until it is reduced to 2 cups. Pick the meat from the bones, discarding fat, gristle, and bones. Pack the meat in a bowl and pour over it the reduced liquor. Leave in a cool place to set. When cold and firm, scrape off any fat which may have settled on top and turn out the brawn onto a plate.

Cock of the North

Ingredients: 1 4-pound capon, 4 tablespoons flour, ½ pound bacon, diced; ¾ cup Irish whiskey, ½ teaspoon allspice, 1 cup water, 1 pound mushrooms, 2 tablespoons light cream, juice of 2 lemons, 1 cup (½ pound) butter, 1 clove garlic, 5 small yellow onions, 1 cup burgundy, 1 pound pearl onions, 2 egg yolks, salt and pepper.

Method: Cut up the capon as for fricassee. Dip the pieces in lemon juice and then in 3 tablespoons seasoned flour. Brown in butter. Add bacon and small yellow onions, sprinkle with 1 tablespoon flour, and brown again. Flame the capon with Irish whiskey. Add salt, pepper, garlic, and allspice. Cover with burgundy and water and simmer gently 45-60 minutes.

For the sauce make a stock with the neck, feet, and giblets. Strain off the liquor from the bird and add to the stock. Reduce to half by rapid boiling. Thicken with the raw egg yolks and cream.

Serve the capon in a dish garnished with the pearl onions and mushrooms, each cooked separately in water and lemon juice. Pour part of the sauce over the capon and serve the remainder separately.

Coddle

This is Dublin's traditional Saturday night supper. It is guaranteed to prevent a hangover.

Ingredients: 1 pound sliced streaky bacon, ½ pound pork sausages, 2 medium onions, 1 tablespoon minced parsley, 6 medium potatoes.

Method: Remove rind from bacon and cut in 2-inch pieces. Combine with sausages and blanch 6 minutes in boiling water. Slice onions, pare and quarter potatoes. Combine all ingredients in a stewpan, add pepper and salt to taste, and barely cover with cold water. Cover closely and simmer about 45 minutes. The potatoes should be mushy, and the finished dish should be more potage than stew.

Coddled Coneen

Ingredients: 2 young rabbits, 4 slices streaky bacon, 2 medium onions, 2 tablespoons flour, 3 tablespoons butter, 1 cup milk, 1 tablespoon chopped parsley, pepper and salt to taste, 2 tablespoons vinegar.

Method: Cut up the rabbit and soak it for 30 minutes in 2 cups water

mixed with the vinegar. (This will make it look and taste like chicken.)
Rinse well under running water and pat dry in a towel. Melt the butter
over fairly high heat. Coat rabbit in seasoned flour, brown quickly in
butter, place in a casserole, add the chopped bacon (rind removed), parsley,
sliced onions, and boiled milk. Cover and bake 1 hour in a moderate
(375°) oven.

Duckling Rineanna

(For this recipe I am indebted to the prince of Irish cooks, Chef
William Ryan of Shannon Airport.)

Ingredients: 1 duckling (4-5 pounds), 4 large pared and quartered
apples, 1¼ cups breadcrumbs, 1 cup cider, ⅛ teaspoon grated nutmeg,
1 teaspoon chopped parsley, 1 teaspoon chopped fennel, 1 bay leaf, ½
teaspoon salt, ¼ teaspoon pepper, 2 teaspoons flour, 4 tablespoons butter, ½ teaspoon chopped mint, 4 cored apples to garnish, 2 teaspoons
arrowroot.

Method: Pare, core, and quarter 4 apples. Melt 2 tablespoons butter
over slow heat, add apples, and cook until almost tender. Add ½ cup cider
and cook 10 minutes longer. Season with salt and pepper and add parsley,
fennel, and nutmeg. Add enough breadcrumbs to soak up the apple mixture and make a moist but stiff dressing. Stuff prepared duck with apple
mixture. Tie or truss well. Dredge duckling with flour, put it in a roasting
pan, and cook at 450° for 40-45 minutes. Bake the 4 cored apples slowly
for about 25 minutes. When duckling is done, remove it from the liquor
and set it aside to keep hot. Strain off pan liquor into a saucepan, add
remainder of cider, and reduced by quick boiling to half the volume, skim-
ming off fat. Add chopped mint. Thicken with arrowroot diluted with
water or stock, strain again and reheat. Remove twine and skewers from
duckling and place on serving dish with baked apples. Pour sauce over
just before serving.

Griskins

Ingredients: 1 pound griskins (these are the odds and ends of lean pork
which are trimmed off when the pig is being cut up before curing),
1 egg, 1 teaspoon salt, ¼ teaspoon pepper, 1 cup breadcrumbs, 2 tablespoons flour.

Method: Pound the meat thin with a rolling pin, dip it first in seasoned flour, then in beaten egg, and finally in fine breadcrumbs. Fry golden brown in butter or lard. Serve with a sharp dressing made by adding to 1 cup mayonnaise, 1 tablespoon each of chopped raw apple, celery, and onion, and 2 teaspoons minced parsley.

Haslett

In the village where I grew up there was an army pensioner who was as quiet as a lamb except on the day when he drew his pension. Then, after a few drinks, he would stand at the village pump offering to take on all comers. "Who wants haslett?" he would roar. Haslett being the Irish equivalent of the Scotch haggis, this was an invitation to come and be minced.

Ingredients: 1 sheep's head and liver, 1 pound beef suet, 10-12 small onions, ½ pound ground oatmeal, 1 teaspoon allspice, salt and pepper to taste.

Method: Boil the sheep's head and liver until tender. Chop the meat fine, mix with the chopped suet, chopped onions, oatmeal, and seasoning. Add about 2 cups of the liquor in which head and liver were boiled. In Scotland they boil this mixture in the stomach of a freshly killed sheep. In Ireland we prefer to put it in a large greased bowl. This is tied down with several thicknesses of greased brown paper and the haslett is steamed for about 4 hours.

Irish Stew

The original Irish stew was made with spare ribs. Today we make it with mutton.

Ingredients: 2 pounds best end neck of mutton, 3 pounds (9 medium) potatoes, 10-12 small onions, pepper and salt, 2 cups cold water, ½ pound streaky bacon.

Method: Cut the mutton in neat pieces and trim away as much fat as possible. Remove rind from bacon and cut in 1-inch pieces. Pare the potatoes and slice the onions. Place a layer of meat in a heavy stewpan, add a layer of onions and potatoes, sprinkle with seasoning. Repeat layers, finishing with potatoes. Add the water, let it come slowly to a boil, remove any scum, cover, and simmer gently 2½ hours. The potatoes should be cooked to a pulp.

Mutton Pies of Abbeyfeale

These were originally created by the farmers' wives of Abbeyfeale to sustain their husbands on Fair days. But when the local gentry discovered how good they were the pies soon became favorites at point-to-point meetings and shooting-party luncheons.

Ingredients: 1 pound lean mutton, a bouquet garni, 1 medium onion stuck with a clove, 6 peppercorns, ½ cup diced carrot, 2 tablespoons chopped onion, 2 tablespoons diced raw potato, salt and pepper to taste, slightly more than ½ Lardy Cakes recipe (p. 37).

Method: Put the mutton into a stewpan with the bouquet, onion, salt, pepper, and peppercorns. Barely cover with cold water, bring to a boil, skim, and simmer covered until just tender. Allow the meat to cool in the liquor. Put carrot and onion in a pan, add enough of the stock to cover, simmer 5 minutes, and add the potato. Simmer until the vegetables are cooked but still firm.

Drain, reserving the stock, and turn the vegetables into a bowl. Dice the drained cold mutton and combine with the vegetables, adding seasoning to taste and a little stock to moisten. Divide the pastry in half and roll out thinly. Use one half to line muffin tins. Fill with the meat and vegetable mixture. Wet the edges. Use remaining pastry to make lids for the pies. Press edges well together, decorate and brush with beaten egg. Bake 25 minutes in a 425° oven.

Michaelmas Goose

In England the custom of eating a roast goose on Michaelmas Day (September 29) is supposed to date from Elizabethan times. They say that Elizabeth I happened to be dining on roast goose when they brought her news of the defeat of the Spanish Armada. To commemorate the event she ordered that goose be the *plat du jour* each September 29. Whatever the truth of this, there is no doubt that in Ireland the Michaelmas goose had its origin in the tyranny of the landlords. Michaelmas Day was rent day, and the unfortunate tenants always paid a stubble* goose with their rent to propitiate the landlord and in the hope that their rent would not be raised. As an old rhyme puts it:

> And when the tenants came to pay their quarter's rent
> They bring some fowls at Midsummer;
> A dishe of fishe in Lent;
> At Christmas a capon, at Michaelmas a goose,
> And somewhat else at New Year's tide
> For feare their lease flie loose.

Happily, nowadays tenant as well as landlord celebrates St. Michael's Day with a succulent stuffed goose. And this is how it is cooked:

Ingredients: 1 goose (about 8 pounds), 1 lemon, 1 teaspoon salt.

Dressing for crop: 1 cup breadcrumbs, 2 teaspoons chopped parsley, 1 teaspoon thyme, 1 tablespoon chopped celery, 1 tablespoon chopped onion, 1 tablespoon butter, ½ teaspoon grated lemon rind, 1 teaspoon salt, ¼ teaspoon pepper, ¼ teaspoon nutmeg, 2 tablespoons milk.

Dressing for body of goose: 2 cups mashed potatoes, 1 cup boiled chopped onions, 2 teaspoons powdered sage, the chopped boiled liver of the goose, 1 egg, pepper and salt to taste.

Method: Singe and clean the goose, cut off the neck, leaving sufficient skin attached to the body to make a flap to secure the dressing. Wash thoroughly inside and out, first with 4 cups of water containing 1 teaspoon baking soda. Rinse under running water and dry well. Rub the inside of the goose with cut lemon and 1 teaspoon salt. Mix together all ingredients for dressing for the crop and stuff the crop. Turn the flap of skin over the back and secure with a skewer or white sewing cotton. Mix ingredients for dressing for the body of the goose (in Ireland we feel that potato dressing is less greasy than breadcrumb dressing). Bind with beaten egg. Stuff

* Sometimes known as graylag or wild goose. More commonly, it is a goose which has been put to graze in the stubble of the cornfields after the harvest is gathered.

the goose loosely, truss, and secure with skewers. Prick the skin of the goose with a fork or skewer to allow excess fat to run out. Place breast down on a rack in a roasting pan and roast 3 hours at 325°. If the goose is stubborn and shows no sign of browning sufficiently when it has been in the oven 2¼ hours, dredge with flour, baste with pan liquor, and increase the heat to 400°. Serve with brown gravy and apple sauce.

Mock Duck

This can be a tender piece of steak but the traditional Irish mock duck is pork tenderloin.

Ingredients: 2 pork tenderloins (about 1 pound each), 1½ cups poultry dressing, 1 medium cooking apple, 2 tablespoons butter or bacon fat, 1 teaspoon salt, ½ teaspoon pepper, 3 tablespoons chopped onion, 4 rashers streaky bacon, ½ cup stock or water.

Method: Split the tenderloins lengthwise, being careful not to cut through. Pound them with a rolling pin. Spread one of the tenderloins with poultry dressing mixed with pared and chopped apple. Place the other tenderloin on top and tie securely. Brown on all sides quickly in hot butter or bacon fat. Transfer to casserole. Sprinkle with salt and pepper. Cover with chopped onion. Lay the bacon on top so the tenderloin will be self-basting. Add water or stock. Cover and simmer 1½ hours in a moderate (325°) oven. Remove to hot platter. Skim fat from pan liquor and thicken with a walnut of butter kneaded with 1 tablespoon flour. Boil up, simmer 3 minutes, season to taste, and strain. Serve with applesauce or rowanberry jelly.

Partridge Manglam

The best partridges in the world are bred in Ireland, and the best partridges in Ireland are found in the Bog of Allen where I was reared. Here it was that Fionn MacCumhaill and his band of heroes (the Irish counterparts of the Red Branch Knights) once roamed and hunted and performed their feats of valor. In Fionn's day the partridges were roasted on a spit of osier rods over a turf fire. Today we find it more convenient to roast these tasty birds in an electric oven or on top of the cooker. Partridge is better eating when not too high, so a maximum of 7 days' hanging should be allowed.

Ingredients: 2 decent plump partridges, 2 medium onions, 2 medium carrots, 2 tablespoons butter or bacon fat, 1 medium compact cabbage, ¼ pound streaky bacon, ¼ pound pork sausages, a bouquet garni, ¾ cup stock, ¾ cup burgundy, seasoning to taste, 1½ tablespoons butter, 1 tablespoon flour, 2 teaspoons chopped parsley, pepper and salt to taste.

Method: Slice onions and carrots thinly. Heat 2 tablespoons butter or bacon fat in a heavy frying pan. Brown the partridges in the fat. Quarter the cabbage and remove most of the stalk. Blanch with the bacon 5 minutes in boiling water. Remove partridges from the pan; add onions and carrots and sauté until tender but not brown. Drain, rinse, and pat the cabbage dry. Cut each quarter in 3 pieces. Remove rind from bacon and cut in small strips. Joint the birds. Fry the sausages light golden brown in the pan and take them out. Arrange half the cabbage in casserole, cover with bacon, partridges, sausages, onions, and carrots. Add bouquet garni and season well. Top with remaining cabbage, add stock. Tuck in all ingredients with a piece of foil and cover with casserole lid. Cook 2 hours in a slow (325°) oven. To serve, place cabbage with onions and carrots in center of a large platter; arrange partridge on top; ring with sausages and bacon. Reduce pot liquor by one-quarter and thicken with 1½ tablespoons butter kneaded with 1 tablespoon flour. Boil up, simmer 3 minutes. Pour some of this sauce over the dish; serve remainder separately.

Pig's Cheek

Ingredients: Half a pickled pig's head, 6 peppercorns, 2 cups cider, 3 tablespoons fine breadcrumbs.

Method: Singe the cheek and soak 12 hours in cold water. Wash and clean thoroughly. Put to cook in a large saucepan. Add peppercorns, cider, and sufficient cold water to cover. Simmer gently until tender (about 25 minutes to a pound). When done, take up the cheek and place it on a fireproof platter. Score the skin well, sprinkle thickly with breadcrumbs, and toast under the grill. Serve on a bolster of green cabbage.

N.B.: Some cooks like to omit the peppercorns and cider from the cooking water and to add the quartered cabbage about 30 minutes before the cheek is done.

Pig's Puddings

There was a time when the making of black and white pig's puddings were a traditional chore at pig-killing time. The mixture was boiled in the scrupulously cleaned intestines of the pig. Nowadays we find it more convenient to boil the puddings in greased bowls. Recipes vary from county to county. In Kildare we make them this way:

Black Puddings

Ingredients: 4 cups sheep's or pig's blood, 1 pound chopped leaf lard, 2 teaspoons salt, 1 teaspoon pepper, 1½ cups milk, 1½ cups steel-cut oatmeal, 1 cup chopped onions or leeks, 2 cups boiling water, ½ cup flour.

Method: Add 1 teaspoon salt to the blood and keep stirring until dissolved (this is to prevent lumpiness). Add the steel-cut oatmeal to the boiling water and cook, stirring occasionally, for 15 minutes. Strain the blood and add the milk, onions, lard, oatmeal, seasonings, and flour. Place in a large greased bowl or bowls, tie down with greased brown paper, and steam 1 hour. To serve: Cut in slices and fry with bacon for breakfast or supper.

White Puddings

Ingredients: 5 cups flake oatmeal, 2 cups milk; 2 medium onions, parboiled and chopped; ¾ pound chopped leaf lard, ½ pound pork liver, parboiled and minced; 2 teaspoons mixed herbs, 2 teaspoons salt, 1 teaspoon pepper.

Method: Soak the oatmeal overnight in the milk. Combine all ingredients and mix well. Pack in 3 greased bowls, tie down with greased brown paper, and steam 1 hour. Serve like black puddings.

Spiced Beef

This is a Christmas dish. It is usually eaten cold when the Christmas Eve fast ends at midnight, and is a welcome reviver after the work of trimming the tree, filling the stockings, and doing the pre-Christmas Day odds and ends of cooking.

Ingredients: 3 pounds topside beef, 2 onions, 2 carrots, 1 small turnip, 2 stalks celery, 1 tablespoon butter or other fat. For marinade: 2 cups cider, 1 bay leaf, 1 teaspoon each cinnamon, allspice, cloves, and pepper; 1½ teaspoons salt.

Method: Mix spices, bay leaf, pepper, and salt with cider. Place meat in a large dish, pour marinade over and let it stand 12 hours, turning twice. Place meat in a heavy sauce pan. Combine marinade with sufficient water to cover; bring to a boil and pour over meat. Cover closely and simmer 3 hours. The meat may be left to cool and eaten cold. Or it may be served hot with a sauce made as follows: Chop small the onions, carrots, turnip, and celery. Sauté 5 minutes in butter or dripping. Add 1½ cups of liquor from meat and simmer about 10 minutes, or until vegetables are tender. Thicken with 1 tablespoon of butter kneaded with 1 tablespoon of flour.

Statia Dunne's Stew

Ingredients: 2 pounds round steak, 4 stalks celery, 1 white turnip, 2 medium onions, 3 medium carrots, 2 tablespoons bacon fat, 2 tomatoes, 1½ tablespoons flour, 1 teaspoon sugar, ½ teaspoon dry mustard, 1 teaspoon salt, ¼ teaspoon pepper, 1 tablespoon chopped parsley, a bouquet garni, 2 cups stock or water.

Method: Trim meat and cut into 1-inch cubes. Chop celery and onions. Dice carrots and turnip, skin and slice tomatoes. Mix flour with pepper, salt, and dry mustard. Melt bacon fat in frying pan. Roll meat in seasoned flour and brown quickly. Place meat in stewpan. Blend remainder of flour with fat in pan; stir until brown. Add water or stock and sugar and bring to a boil. Pour over meat, add bouquet garni, cover, and simmer 1½ hours. Add vegetables. Simmer until vegetables are tender. Remove bouquet garni. Serve stew in a browned border of mashed potatoes with parsley sprinkled on top.

Trotters

Trotters or crubeens—pig's feet by any name taste just as sweet. They may be bought, steaming hot, in the shops on Saturday evening, but they are much better cooked at home in this way:

Simmer 6 pickled pig's feet until tender in water to which has been added 6 peppercorns tied in muslin, a bouquet garni, 1 medium carrot, sliced; 1 medium onion, sliced; and 2 stalks celery, chopped. They will take about 1½ hours. Split and bone them, then dip in egg and breadcrumbs and fry golden brown in butter or bacon fat. Serve with onion sauce and colcannon (p. 74).

Venison

There is a Munster proverb which advises against "bheith ag ithe na feola fiadh agus an fheoil-fhiadh ar an gnoc go foill" (eating your venison while the deer is still on the mountain). For many of us the deer will remain in their mountain haunts. But just in case a haunch of venison should one day find its way into your kitchen, this is how you should cook it.

Hang the venison for 2-3 weeks in a cool airy place, rubbing it over each day with a dry cloth. Wash it in warm water and dry with a cloth. Smear it all over with dripping, wrap in thickly greased brown paper, and then envelop it in a stiff flour and water paste. Wrap it again in greased paper and tie with string. Weigh the vension and place in a hot (450°) oven. Allow 20 minutes to a pound and baste frequently. Thirty minutes before the haunch is cooked, take it from the oven, remove paper and paste, dredge with flour, and return to the oven to brown delicately. Serve with brown gravy and with red currant sauce made as follows: Simmer ½ cup port wine and ½ cup cider with a bouquet garni until reduced by half. Stir in 2 tablespoons red currant jelly. Reheat and serve at once. Venison should be served on very hot plates as the fat chills quickly.

TRIPE

There are people in Ireland who would nearly as soon miss Mass as go without their Sunday breakfast of tripe and onions. When my poor Gran was in her dotage and barely able to put one foot past the other, we thought we'd give her a treat one Wednesday morning. A breakfast of the tripe and onions she loved was taken to her in bed. Half an hour later she appeared dressed in her Sunday finery of jet-trimmed cape and little black bonnet with its satin ribbons tied under her chin. Missal in hand she demanded, "Well, are ye ready to take me to Mass?" "But, sure this is only Wednesday, Gran," we explained.

Bewilderment clouded her little creased face. "If that's the case, why did I get tripe for my breakfast?" she asked aggrievedly.

Tripe and Onions

Ingredients: 1½ pounds tripe, 4 cups milk, 4 medium onions, 1 teaspoon salt, ¼ teaspoon pepper, 4 tablespoons butter, ½ cup flour.

Method: Cut tripe in strips about 3 by 1½ inches. Place in casserole with sliced onions, salt, pepper, and boiled milk. Cover and cook about 2 hours at 300°. When ready to serve, melt butter in saucepan over low heat, stir in flour, and cook until it forms a paste, taking care not to let it brown. Gradually add milk stock from tripe, bring to a boil, stir well, and simmer 3 minutes. Pour over tripe and serve with toast.

Tripe Pie

Ingredients: 2 cups poundies (potatoes mashed with butter and cream or milk), 2 pounds honeycomb tripe (bought prepared from butcher), 2 cups water, 2 tablespoons vinegar, 1 medium onion, 4 cloves, 1 teaspoon salt, ¼ teaspoon pepper, 4 tablespoons butter, 2 tablespoons flour, 1 egg.

Method: Cut tripe in 2-inch squares. Place in saucepan and add water, vinegar, chopped onion, cloves, salt, and pepper. Melt butter over low heat in another pan; add flour and stir well. Put into the saucepan in which tripe is cooking. Cook an additional 5 minutes, stirring constantly. Turn the tripe into a casserole, with a pastry tube pipe a thick border of poundies around the edge, brush with beaten egg, and place in a hot (425°) oven until potatoes are nicely browned.

8

Fast-Day Feasts

"... you shall eat the good things of the land."

Isias I, 19

EGGS, CHEESE, CEREALS

*I*n my mind nested eggs will always be linked up with the homecoming of Nora Neelan.

It was a Friday in Lent. For our dinner we were having baked eggs set in a nest of mashed potatoes, with buttered carrots on the side. That was always a popular fast-day dinner in our house. Living so far inland, we rarely had fish. My mother had so many lovely ways of cooking eggs that we did not miss it.

On that particular Friday I had been getting under my mother's feet in the kitchen, and she sent me out in the street to play until the dinner would be ready. I stayed near the door, spanceled (tethered) by the smell from the kitchen, and torturing my clamoring stomach with thoughts of the tasty plateful which eventually would be set before me.

My gluttonous thoughts were diverted by the sight of old Mary Neelan coming out to call her hens. Her house was right opposite ours. I had often heard the grownups talk about Mary's tragedy.

It seemed that twenty-five years before, Mary's only daughter, Nora, was in service in Dublin when she met and married a well-off man. Nora was such a lovely girl that no one was surprised. She came home for the wedding. The style of it was the talk of the place. "Isn't it well for Mary Neelan that her daughter made such a good match?" people said. "With a wealthy son-in-law, she'll never see a poor day."

For a year it seemed as if they were right. Letters with a London postmark came regularly from Nora, and nearly every letter contained a postal order.

Then all at once the letters stopped. Nora had left her London home. After the move she never again wrote to her mother. Hard things were said about her for neglecting the old woman while she herself lived on the fat of the land. "Although it isn't the money Mary Neelan misses," my mother said, "it's the news of her daughter. She always adored her."

That must be a lonely thing, I thought, as I watched old Mary. To be old and a widow and never to get a letter from your daughter— that must be a very lonely thing.

"Here, chuck-chuck-chuck!" she called. On the "Here," her voice rose in a wild despairing pleading. It fell to a soft coaxing on the "chuck-chuck-chuck." "Here, chuck-chuck-chuck." Come to think of it, the old woman resembled a hen. Her arms and face and hair had the faded gingeriness of a Rhode Island Red. Her heavy bosoms hung to her waist on each side like folded wings. Being nearsighted, she gave her head a little upward jerk as she peered from side to side, for all the world like a hen drinking.

The fowl came swishing from all directions, their horny toes making a sound like untied bootlaces as they skeetered over the hard road. With hoarse, greedy clucks they attacked the few handfuls of oats she scattered.

Mary was turning to go into her house when Graham's bread van

from Kildare pulled up right at her door. Out of it stepped a woman,
a tired-looking, graying woman, poorly dressed.

Mrs. Neelan and she stood looking at each other. "Don't you know
me, Mother?" I heard the stranger say.

Mrs. Neelan gave a little cry. "Nora! It's Nora's voice!" For another minute they stood there, while the old woman shook her head
unbelievingly. "Me little girl," she said. "Me lovely little girl!" Just
then I was called in to my nested eggs and I did not see any more.

But later I heard my mother and my aunt talking about Nora's
home-coming.

"Wasn't she the foolish poor child," said my mother, "to cut herself off from everyone when that go-boy of a husband cleared out and
left her without a penny?"

"Don't be talking," said my Aunt Julia. "Pride is responsible for
many a sorrow. But I think she had every right to warn her mother
when she decided to come home. Mary Neelan might have died of the
shock."

"Small fear of it," my mother retorted. "No one ever died of joy."
Which, of course, is very true.

Even though we live in an island ringed by seas and veined by
rivers which abound in fish, we Irish are not a fish-eating people. In
fact, in times past, the laborers of Connaught insisted that their work
contract should include a clause prohibiting the serving of boiled
salmon for dinner more than twice a week. (That, of course, was in
the days when the fish in the rivers were there for the taking and
before angling licenses were necessary.) Still, as an appetizer for a
fast-day meal we often serve "whets" and this is one of the best of them.

Anchovy Whet

Ingredients: 6 thick slices of bread, 1 egg, ½ cup milk, 4 tablespoons
butter, 6 anchovies, ½ cup grated cheese, 2 tablespoons chopped parsley,
2 tablespoons melted butter.

Method: Cut crusts from bread, dip lightly in beaten egg and milk, fry golden brown in butter. Lay an anchovy on each slice of bread, sprinkle with cheese, parsley, and melted butter. Place under grill until cheese melts and browns.

Blarney Puffballs

Ingredients: 2 cups riced potatoes, 2 eggs, 4 tablespoons cream, salt and pepper to taste, a dust of cayenne, ½ cup grated cheese, ½ teaspoon minced parsley, deep fat for frying.

Method: Keep the potatoes hot. Separate eggs. Beat yolks and add to cream. Mix with potato, cheese, and seasonings. Beat the egg whites stiff and fold gently into the potato mixture. Drop by tablespoonfuls into hot fat and fry golden brown. Drain on a paper towel and serve with buttered peas and carrots.

Bread and Cheese Panada

Ingredients: 2 cups grated Cheddar cheese, 4 cups breadcrumbs, 2 cups milk, 2 eggs, 1 teaspoon salt, ½ teaspoon pepper, 2 tablespoons butter.

Method: Mix together cheese, crumbs, pepper, and salt. Boil the milk and pour it over them. When the mixture is cold, beat in the eggs. Put into a deep buttered dish, dot the top with butter, and bake until golden brown in a 400° oven.

Dunmurry Rice

Ingredients: 1 cup rice, 2 cups white stock, 4 tablespoons chopped onions, 4 tablespoons butter, 1 cup sliced mushrooms, 1 teaspoon salt, ½ teaspoon pepper, 4 tomatoes, 2 teaspoons minced parsley.

Method: Melt 2 tablespoons butter over low heat and cook onion until transparent but not brown. Stir in rice, incorporating well with butter and onions. Add stock and seasonings. Cover and cook slowly until rice is tender and dry (giving an occasional shake to the pot to prevent burning). Melt remaining 2 tablespoons butter in a frying pan. Add mushrooms, cover, and cook gently about 10 minutes. Add to the rice. Pack mixture into a heated greased bowl, leave 5 minutes in a hot place, turn out onto a hot platter, and serve wreathed with parsley-sprinkled grilled tomato halves.

Egg Collops

Ingredients: 4 hard-cooked eggs, ½ cup thick white sauce (made with cream), 3 tablespoons fine breadcrumbs, 2 beaten eggs, 2 tablespoons grated cheese, pepper and salt to taste, 2 tablespoons flour. Garnish: buttered peas and buttered parslied carrots.

Method: Shell and chop the hard-cooked eggs. Add pepper and salt, grated cheese, and white sauce. Bind with a little beaten egg to a stiff paste. With floured hands, form the mixture into cork shapes. Roll in beaten egg and then in breadcrumbs. Fry golden brown in hot fat. Serve piled on a platter and ringed with alternating mounds of buttered peas and buttered parslied carrots.

Friday Manglam

Ingredients: 4 cups well-seasoned potato mashed with butter, cream, and a sprinkling of chopped onion and minced parsley; 4 eggs, 2 large tomatoes, 2 tablespoons grated cheese, 2 tablespoons breadcrumbs, pepper and salt, 2 tablespoons butter.

Method: Put mashed potato in a well-greased pie dish. Make 8 wells in the potato. Into every second well, break a raw egg carefully. In the others, place a halved tomato, cut side up. Season lightly with pepper and salt, sprinkle with combined cheese and breadcrumbs, dot with butter, and bake 20 minutes in a moderate (375°) oven.

Golden Vale Pudding

In the southwest of Ireland, there is an area known as the Golden Vale. Here the milch cows graze to sleekness on lush green grass, and their milk is still as rich and as valuable as in the days when St. Patrick pronounced the harming of a milch cow to be one of the three cardinal crimes. In the twelfth century an Irish poet composed *The Triads of Ireland,* a collection of "Threes" into which he condensed the wisdom of the world. They still hold good today, particularly the Triad which says, "Three places where the world is made new: woman's womb, cow's udder, smith's anvil." Because of the richness of the milk from the Golden Vale we value particularly the cheese which bears this name.

Ingredients: 1 cup fine breadcrumbs, ¾ cup grated Golden Vale cheddar cheese, 3 eggs, 3 cups milk, 2 tablespoons butter, salt and cayenne to taste, ¼ recipe for Apple Cake Pastry (p. 43), omitting sugar and lemon peel.

Method: Boil the milk, pour over butter, breadcrumbs, and seasonings. Stir until butter is dissolved and leave 30 minutes, or until cold. Separate eggs. Reserve 1 tablespoon beaten egg yolk. Beat remainder into milk mixture. Add grated cheese. Fold in stiffly beaten egg whites. Line a flan tin, or other shallow baking dish with the thinly rolled shortcrust pastry, making a fluted edge. Brush edge with beaten egg yolk. Fill flan with cheese mixture and bake 40 minutes in a moderate (375°) oven.

Golden Vale Ramekins

Ingredients: 2 eggs, ½ cup grated Golden Vale Cheddar cheese, ½ cup cream or milk, 3 tablespoons butter, 2 teaspoons flour, pepper and salt to taste.

Method: Mix together cheese and beaten eggs, add flour blended with cream or milk. Add seasoning to taste. Mix in melted butter. Pour mixture into buttered muffin tins. Stand the tins in a baking dish containing hot water and oven-poach until the ramekins are golden brown and firm.

N.B.: You will have no difficulty in buying Golden Vale cheese in America. It is one of Ireland's best dollar-earners.

Maeve Cheese Fries

This is a good way to use up odds and ends of dry cheese. The dish gets its name from the story which tells of the ignominious death of Maeve, the warlike Queen of Connaught. The woman who led thousands of men to victory was taking her ease in her garden one day. Her nephew, whom she had offended, was keeping an eye on her from behind a hazel hedge. The lad was eating his lunch which consisted of oaten bread and a piece of hard cheese. On a sudden, vindictive impulse he fitted the lump of cheese into his catapult and took a potshot at his aunt. The piece of cheese hit the poor woman on the temple and she dropped dead on the spot.

Ingredients: 4 slices bread (about ¼-inch thick), 2 tablespoons butter, ½ cup grated hard cheese, ½ cup processed or cream cheese, ½ teaspoon paprika, 1 clove garlic (crushed), ½ teaspoon caraway seeds, pinch of black pepper, 2 chopped shallots or spring onions, 1 egg, bacon fat or butter for frying.

Method: Cream 1 tablespoon butter, add grated cheese, cream cheese, garlic, and seasonings, beating well until smooth. Chop the shallots or onions, add to the remaining butter, and fold into the cheese mixture. Spread this filling on 2 slices of bread, cover with the other two, pressing well together. Cut in halves or quarters, brush with beaten egg, and fry golden brown in butter or bacon fat.

Mealie Greachie

On fast days this is served as an accompaniment to the fried breakfast eggs. Melt 2 tablespoons butter or bacon fat in frying pan. Add as much flake oatmeal as will absorb the fat, and fry until the meal is toasted. Some people like to include a little chopped onion.

Mount Mellary Eggs

Trim and boil 12 good-sized Jerusalem artichokes and leave them to cool. Chop 6 hard-cooked eggs. Slice the artichokes and place in a buttered pie dish, add a layer of chopped eggs and then a layer of skinned sliced tomatoes. Each layer should be well seasoned and dotted with scraps of butter. Top with a good sprinkling of grated cheese and bake 30 minutes in a moderate (375°) oven.

Nested Eggs

For each person allow ¾ cup potato mashed with butter and cream, 1 tablespoon cooked peas, 1 egg, 2 teaspoons butter.

Method: Place the potatoes in mounds on a greased baking sheet. Press a cup into each to make a hollow. Place a tablespoon of cooked peas in each "nest," carefully break a raw egg over the peas. Season with pepper and salt and dot with butter. Brush with beaten egg and bake 20 minutes in a 375° oven. Serve with buttered parslied carrots.

9

Sauces, Sweet and Savory

"...of a most sweet savor..."
Leviticus III, 16

*T*he Foleys were nearly a year married before Sheila discovered that a wife's first duty to her husband is to cook him the kind of meals he likes, and that no marriage can be really happy unless a man is satisfied with his table treatment.

They started with everything in their favor. They were young, healthy, and good-looking. The public house which Dan had inherited from his uncle brought them an adequate living. And they were wildly in love.

They had been in love from the very first minute they laid eyes on each other. That was when Sheila, who had been sent down by the Department to lecture on bee-keeping, went into Dan's grocery-hardware-drapery-confectionery-saloon looking for a jar of stuffed olives. Dan was not able to supply the olives, but he was able to give Sheila the kind of love of which she had always dreamed. Three months later he gave her a wedding ring.

Sheila's trouble was that she had been brought up by two refined maiden aunts who believed that if you had enough cutlery, glass, and lace mats on the table nothing else mattered. Their idea of a good square meal was a triangle of toast trimmed with a dab of dressed crab and a sprig of parsley.

For the first few months of his marriage Dan Foley was too drunk with love to know or care what he was eating. In fact, with Sheila sitting across the table from him it is doubtful if he would have been able to tackle anything more substantial than the celery curls with cheese soufflé which she called dinner. I will go further and say that if, during that first fine careless rapture, Dan had caught Sheila's smile while he was coping with a mouthful of steak or ham it is probable that the man would have choked. If now and again he felt a certain emptiness, a peculiar gnawing, he wrote it off as the debilitating effect of love.

Now, prolonged hunger can have two effects. If a man has the qualities which turn monks into saints, fast and abstinence can drive out the devil. If, like Dan Foley, he is just an ordinary, decent, hard-working husband, hunger is more likely to bring out everything that's bad in him.

The young couple were barely six months married when Dan, to his horror, found himself snapping at Sheila one morning when she asked him a simple question. It happened just as she put his breakfast before him—two sardines beautifully arranged on a postage stamp of toast.

Sheila burst into tears, whereupon Dan naturally acknowledged that he was a brute and a cruel, insensitive monster. They kissed and made up, Dan swearing never again to offend.

But he did offend, again and again and again. Day by day he grew more peevish and snappy. But not realizing that these faults were but the symptoms of semistarvation, a hurt and bewildered Sheila became convinced that her husband did not love her. Having her share of pride, she became cold and distant.

On the Saturday night Jim Regan called into Dan's pub for a pint of porter, the marriage was well on its way to being wrecked.

Jim had a parcel under his arm. "I can hardly wait for tomorrow's dinner," he said. "I've a pig's cheek here that's as plump as any I ever saw. With plenty of green cabbage and floury spuds it will make sweet eating."

Dan stopped dead in the act of drawing the pint. He had just come down from a tea of petit fours and watercress sandwiches which had done nothing to fill the void left by a dinner of sweetbreads with a dessertspoon of creamed potato and a teaspoon of peas. "Pig's cheek?" he echoed faintly. He pictured it smoking hot, the tender lean marbled with pearly fat. He pictured it cold, its firm nuttiness emphasized by the sharpness of pickled onions. He swallowed. Slowly, he handed the pint across the counter. "It's years since I tasted pig's cheek," he said wistfully.

Jim Regan took a long drink. "We have one every Sunday," he confided. "We both like pig's cheek so much that we'd nearly need two of them—though I remember the time Mary wouldn't look at it. She had vegetarian notions when we married—used to serve me up nut rissoles, I thank you! But I soon put a stop to that. I went home to my mother for dinner every day until I brought her to her senses. Since then we've never had a sharp word." He finished his pint. "Aye, indeed," he said. "A woman won't ever be happy till you let her see who's boss."

Dan Foley was never slow to act on good advice. He took a pound note from the till. "Do me a favor, Jim." His eyes were the eyes of a man who has seen the truth, and his voice was determined. "Step over to Murphy's and get me the fellow of that pig's cheek."

"You should have told me," was what Sheila said with tender reproach. "Didn't you know well I'd give you my heart for your dinner if I thought you fancied it?"

But Sheila did not confine her cooking to unadorned hearty dishes. She learned to combine substance with savor. And by increasing her repertoire of sauces, she was able to indulge her own taste for classy cooking while enhancing her husband's enjoyment of satisfying food.

And that is the whole point of a good sauce—to enhance and improve the food it accompanies.

SAVORY SAUCES

Game Sauce

Ingredients: 1 cup port wine, 1 cup good brown gravy, 2 tablespoons minced shallot, 1 teaspoon salt, ½ teaspoon pepper, ¼ teaspoon grated nutmeg, a pinch of ground mace, 1½ tablespoons butter, 1 tablespoon flour.

Method: Combine all ingredients except butter and flour and simmer 10 minutes. Stir in butter kneaded with flour, cook another 3 minutes, strain and serve.

Mayonnaise (Foolproof)

Is there any culinary mishap more disheartening than curdled mayonnaise, or mayonnaise which refuses to thicken? To prevent this misfortune and preserve your good humor, try making mayonnaise this way:

Ingredients: 1 raw egg yolk, 1 hard-cooked egg yolk, 1 cup olive oil, 2 tablespoons vinegar, ½ teaspoon dry mustard, 1 teaspoon salt.

Method: Mix seasonings and egg yolks to a paste. Gradually add the oil, beating well after each addition. As you come toward the last of the oil, alternate with vinegar.

You can work all kinds of variations into this basic mayonnaise. For instance, a very piquant dressing for serving with meat, fish, chicken, and egg salads may be made by adding a couple of tablespoons of finely chopped pickles and ½ tablespoon of minced parsley. A few tablespoons of finely chopped crisp celery and/or cucumber is another good addition. Or you might try a tablespoon of minced chives. A tablespoon of sharp grated cheese is good, too.

Mushroom Ketchup

Let folks say what they like, there is nothing to equal homemade mushroom ketchup. A word of warning: if kept longer than 12 months it will ferment and become as heady as champagne. On one occasion, when my mother, who hated waste, emptied two bottles of fermented ketchup into the hens' food, the White Wyandottes and Rhode Island Reds staggered about for days with the father-and-mother of a hangover.

Gather the mushrooms as you find them—the large flat juicy kind which we call "platters" are best. Break the mushrooms in pieces, put them in a deep earthenware crock or bowl (a metal container is not suitable), and sprinkle with salt, allowing 4 tablespoons salt to each pound of mushrooms. Leave them for 3 or 4 days, and stir a couple of times daily. Then place the bowl in a very slow oven, cover it, and cook the mushrooms 1 hour. Strain off the liquor. To each quart add ¼ teaspoon each whole allspice, ground ginger, and peppercorns; ½ teaspoon cloves, and ½ teaspoon each cinnamon and mace. Simmer spiced liquor until it is reduced to half the original quantity. Strain and pour while still hot into hot sterilized bottles. Seal at once. A tablespoonful of mushroom ketchup added to soup, sauce, or stew gives a wonderful meaty zest.

For success in storing care must be taken in sterilizing the bottles. Boil the bottles in a large pan of clean water and fill them with hot sauce just as soon as they are drained. Boil corks for 15 minutes before they are used. If you wish to make really sure that your mushroom ketchup will keep for a year, sterilize the filled bottles. When corked, stand them on a rack or cloth in a pan of simmering water, taking care that the bottles do not touch. Simmer 30 minutes, then take out the bottles and let them cool as when bottling fruit.

Onion Sauce

Dean Swift, author of *Gulliver's Travels* and founder of St. Patrick's Hospital, Dublin (the world's first humane hospital for the mentally ill), liked to collect street vendors' cries. Here is the cry of the Dublin onion-seller:

> Come, follow me by the smell,
> Here are delicate onions to sell,

I promise to use you well
   They make the blood warmer,
   You'll feed like a farmer;
For this is every cook's opinion:
No savory dish without an onion.*

But, lest your kissing should be spoiled,
Your onions must be thoroughly boiled.
   Or else you may spare
   Your mistress a share,
Your secret will never be known:
   She cannot discover
   The breath of her lover,
But think it as sweet as her own.

This onion sauce goes well with steamed lamb or mutton or with boiled ling (salt cod). With sippets of toast and hard-cooked eggs, it is a good supper dish.

Ingredients: 1 cup milk, ¼ cup cream, 2 tablespoons butter, 1½ table-spoon flour, 2 large onions, pepper and salt to taste.

Method: Skin the onions, put them in cold water, bring to the boil and strain. Return to the saucepan with ½ teaspoon salt and sufficient boiling water to cover. Simmer until tender. Drain well and chop coarsely. Melt the butter over moderate heat, stir in the flour, and cook (without browning) for 3 minutes. Add milk gradually and stir until it boils. Add the chopped onions, season to taste, cook for 2 minutes, then add cream.

Plum Ketchup

Ingredients: 4 pounds plums, 1 cup chopped onion, 1 cup sugar, ½ cup currants, 4 cups white vinegar, 2 tablespoons salt, 1 tablespoon dry mustard, 2 teaspoons each ground ginger and allspice; 1 teaspoon each ground nutmeg and turmeric powder.

Method: Cut up the plums and cook with onions in 2 cups of vinegar 30 minutes. Rub the pulp through a sieve; add remaining ingredients and

---

* When spoken, this rhymes better than when written. Many of us in Ireland pronounce onion "ingyin."

simmer 1 hour, stirring occasionally. Bottle and sterilize as for mushroom ketchup (p. 106).

Red Currant Sauce

Ingredients: 1 cup brown gravy, 1 tablespoon lemon juice, 2 tablespoons red currant jelly, 1 tablespoon butter, 1 teaspoon sugar, 1 teaspoon salt, ¼ teaspoon pepper, few grains cayenne.

Method: Add to brown gravy all ingredients except butter. Simmer 2 minutes, stir in butter. Serve with roast lamb.

Sauce for Cold Fowl or Game

Ingredients: Yolks of 2 hard-cooked eggs, 1 anchovy, 2 tablespoons olive oil, 3 tablespoons cider vinegar, 1 chopped shallot, 1 teaspoon dry mustard, 1 teaspoon salt, pinch of cayenne.

Method: Pound all ingredients except oil and vinegar in a mortar. Gradually incorporate oil, then mix in vinegar.

SWEET SAUCES

Brandy Sauce (or Hard Sauce)

Ingredients: ½ cup (¼ pound) butter, 1¾ cups sieved confectioner's sugar, 2 tablespoons cream, 1 teaspoon lemon extract, 2 tablespoons rum or brandy.

Method: Cream the butter until soft, then beat in the sugar gradually and continue beating until light and fluffy. Add the flavoring and cream. Leave in refrigerator overnight. Just before serving, stir in the brandy.

N.B.: This is a "must" with Christmas Pudding.

Chocolate Mist

Ingredients: 1 egg, ½ teaspoon vanilla, ½ cup brown sugar, ½ cup grated cooking chocolate, 1 cup cream.

Method: Separate egg. Beat 2 tablespoons sugar into yolk. Beat egg white until stiff and fold in remainder of sugar. Combine the two mixtures, place in top of double boiler. Add cream and grated chocolate, beating well as it cooks. Remove from heat and add vanilla. Plain baked or steamed puddings cease to be plain when served with this sauce.

Custard Sauce

Of the gang of youngsters who make the roof of my garage their base for forays into Indian territory, outer space, and the neighbors' orchards, I particularly like the stolid and moon-faced urchin who answers to the name of Custhard Gob. I have been told that his insatiable passion for custard earned him his nickname. Who is to blame him? A well-made custard sauce is very delectable—particularly when it is made with cream instead of milk.

Ingredients: 1 cup milk or cream, 1 teaspoon vanilla, 2 tablespoons sugar, 2 eggs.

Method: Scald milk or cream, add flavoring and sugar and stir until sugar is dissolved. Add beaten eggs and cook over hot water, stirring constantly, until sauce is thickened.

N.B.: The mixture must not be allowed to approach boiling point or it will curdle.

Feast-Day Sauce

Ingredients: ½ cup sugar, ½ cup water, 1 cup cream, 1 tablespoon brandy, 1 tablespoon orange-flower water.

Method: Make caramel by boiling sugar and water together until amber in color. Heat cream and add to the caramel, a little at a time, beating well until thoroughly blended. Remove from heat and stir in brandy and orange-flower water. Use for coating cupcakes or individual batter puddings, or for turning any plain pudding into a treat.

N.B.: Especially good served hot with ice cream.

Shannon Foam

Ingredients: 1 cup cream or unsweetened evaporated milk, ¼ cup butter, ½ teaspoon vanilla, ½ teaspoon grated lemon rind, 1 egg white, ¾ cup sifted confectioner's sugar.

Method: Cream butter and sugar. Beat in flavorings and evaporated milk or cream. Fold this mixture into stiffly beaten egg white. Rounds of sponge cake or gingerbread topped with this sauce make a quick and delicious sweet.

Tara Sauce

Ingredients: 2 tablespoons hot water, 4 tablespoons honey, 2 tablespoons minced candied orange and lemon peel, 2 tablespoons chopped hazelnuts.

Method: Combine ingredients and mix well. This is a quickly prepared sauce which will do big things for a plain butter, suet, or cereal pudding. Or for a quick dessert, serve it with pancakes. For a really fancy party dessert, serve the sauce, cold, with ice cream.

Whiskey Sauce

Ingredients: 3 eggs, ½ cup sugar, ½ cup Irish whiskey.

Method: Place all ingredients in top of double boiler and cook, whipping briskly, for 7 or 8 minutes, or until sauce is light and foamy. Very good with sweet omelettes, soufflés, and hot sponge puddings.

10

Jellies, Jams, Pickles

"I went down into the garden of nuts, to see the fruits of the valleys . . ."
Canticle of Canticles VI, 10

*M*y mother made lovely blackberry jelly. We used to gather the black-berries in Doran's wood.

I remember coming home from school one autumn day and rushing into my mother's workroom. She was a dressmaker. "Can Peig and me gather blackberries for jelly?" I asked her.

"You can, to be sure," my mother said. "But don't stay out too late. I don't want Peig catching cold on me." She held up a frilly filmy dress of palest rose. She beckoned to my sister. "Come here, alanna. I want to see how this looks on you. I made it for you out of a bit of stuff I had left over out of Celia Twomey's wedding dress."

My sister took off her school dress and my mother helped her into that lovely dress with its satin bows of baby ribbon and its edgings of fine cream lace. Peig stood there in her finery, her adoring eyes fixed on my mother's face. The soft frills of the dress disguised her painful thinness, and her paleness borrowed a flush from the misty pink material. Although only nine, she was as tall as I who was a year and a half older.

"You'll do," my mother said with satisfaction. "There's no denying that pink is your color."

Pink is my color, too, I wanted to scream. *Didn't Aunt Julia say that pink suited me when she gave me the pink sweater for Christmas?* But I said nothing.

My mother put her arm around Peig and gave her a hug which had a kind of desperation in it. As I stood watching them the old jealousy rose in me like a vomit, and I had to turn away. "I'll get the can for the blackberries," I said, running out of the room.

Doran's wood was ruddy-rich with autumn. The rowan trees dripped sealing wax through their ferny leaves, and the elders were heavy with wine-purple beads. Toadstools like queer jungle dwellings, mottled and sulphur-yellow and brown, ringed the elephant-gray trunks of the chestnuts. Full dark berries winked among the papery leaves of the brambles.

It was a happy place. Any place with my sister Peig was a happy place for me when my mother was not with us. It was not that I did not love my mother. In truth, I loved her too much. That was why to see her with my sister Peig made me unhappy.

My mother loved Peig more than she loved me. Or maybe she didn't. Maybe it was my sister's delicacy that made her yearn over her. She had had a hard fight to keep Peig alive. The pretty clothes she made for her, the special tidbits she cooked for her, the extra caresses and cuddlings—maybe these were her thank offerings to Peig for staying with us in spite of the way her recurring sicknesses pulled the child toward Heaven.

That is how I see it now. But in those other days my jealous heart knew only that my mother favored my sister. There were times when I hated Peig for it. And I hated having to hate my sister, gentle and loving Peig.

That evening in the wood, I was able to lay down for a time the burden of my jealousy. I was even able to forget the pink dress.

Peig came toward me. She carried a full mug so carefully that her little sharp-featured face was old with anxiety. Her thin hair had something of the pale moon-gold of her skin, so that it was hard to tell where her fringe left off and her forehead began.

She tumbled the glittering berries into the can. "It's getting late," she said. "Shouldn't we be going home?"

"Ah, not for another while," I urged. "Sure, the can isn't half full yet."

"But we promised," Peig insisted. "Mother will be worrying in case I catch cold."

At this reminder of my mother's solicitude for my sister, my happiness left. "You can go if you like," I said roughly. "Goody-goody . . . always making sure of being the pet!" Spitefully, I added, "I wish you had seen yourself in the pink dress. You're a holy show in it—like a maypole!"

Peig looked at me in a troubled way. Then she went off from me through the trees.

I continued to pick. But all the joy and all the color had gone out of the wood. There was a bitter heaviness in my heart as I counted my grievances over and over, coming each time with a sick surge of rancor to the latest and greatest of them: the pink dress.

Mrs. Doran came through her garden gate and along the path toward me, but I didn't notice her until she was right beside me. She had to address me twice before I took in what she was saying.

"Isn't it late for you to be out by yourself?" she said. "Is there nobody with you? I thought I heard voices."

"It was my sister," I told her. "She went home."

Mrs. Doran was a rich and lonely woman whose children were all gone from her. She looked at me with kind, tired eyes. Maybe some of the dark hurt I was feeling showed in my face. Suddenly she said. "How would you like to come and have tea with me next Sunday—and your sister? You could play with the doll's house. And I'd find you some books to take home."

Once, on a never-to-be-forgotten evening, Peig and I had been in Mrs. Doran's house. We had been given the run of the dusty nursery, a treasure house of old-fashioned fascinating toys.

With Mrs. Doran's invitation, delight returned momentarily to the wood. "Oh, I'd love that, Mrs. Doran! and Peig——" I stopped short. *And Peig would love it, too,* was what I had been about to say, but my jealous heart put other words into my mouth. "Peig wouldn't be able to come," I lied. "She is going to Kildare with my mother on Sunday."

"Well, come yourself, then," Mrs. Doran said. "Around four."

When she had gone, I stayed there for a little while. The shadows grew longer and the wood started to close in on itself. But I was conscious of nothing but my fierce exultation in having scored over Peig. In advance, I savored the envy that would fill her face when I should tell her that I was going to have tea with Mrs. Doran.

"Serve her right!" I gloated. "Her and her pink dress!"

"Don't make a word of noise," my mother warned me when, my supper eaten, I started up the stairs for bed. "Peig's asleep. Don't waken her on the peril of your life."

I went into the room which I shared with my sister. In the dim red light of the lamp which burned before the Sacred Heart she looked like a dead child who had drowned happily in a pool of sacramental wine.

When I got into bed I wakened Peig. She raised herself on her little pointed elbow and looked at me sleepily. The frightening malice of my jealousy must have shown in my eyes because she shrank back a little.

"You think you're great with your pink dress," I jeered. "Wait till you hear this. I met Mrs. Doran and she asked me to go to tea on Sunday. Just me, do you hear? You're not asked."

I waited to see my sister's face become ugly with envy. Instead, a terrible thing happened. The small, sharp face became soft and round with pleasure—pleasure for me.

"Isn't it well for you?" she breathed wistfully. "You'll have a lovely time." Eagerly, she added, "And you can wear my new pink dress."

A curiously weak and empty feeling came over me.

"The dress will look grand on you," Peig said happily. "That's because your hair is nicer than mine."

I lay down and turned my back to her. "Shut up and let me go to sleep," I said gruffly. But I could hardly bring out the words because of the way my throat was hurting.

JELLIES

These are rules I have found worth following when making jellies:

1. Pick over fruit carefully and cut away any damaged part.
2. Simmer fruit very slowly to extract juice.
3. When straining, leave the fruit until the last drop of juice has dripped from it. Never squeeze the jelly bag if you want clear jelly.
4. Use a thick, close-meshed jelly bag. Failing a real jelly bag, improvise one by tying a double linen or flannelette cloth to the legs of an upturned chair. Place a large bowl beneath to catch the juice.
5. Make sure the sugar has been heated for a few minutes in slow oven before adding it to the juice. (This also applies to jams.)
6. There are several ways of testing jelly to determine whether or not it will set. Among them (1) It should "sheet" when dropped from a spoon; that is, a spoonful when held above the pan and allowed to drop back into it flattens as it drops into a thin sheet which falls away from the edge of the spoon, leaving it more or less clean. Or (2) dropped onto a very cold plate, and left for a minute or two the surface should ripple when touched.

Apple Jelly

Ingredients: Windfall apples, water or cider, 2 lemons and 3 cloves for each 5 pounds apples, 1 cup sugar to each cup of juice.

Method: Wash and cut up apples. Put them in a kettle (peels and cores included) with almost enough water or cider to cover. Simmer until pulpy.

Strain through a jelly bag. Measure and place the juice in preserving pan with strained lemon juice and with rind and cloves tied in muslin. Boil 15 minutes. Remove muslin bag. Add heated sugar, and stir until dissolved. Bring to a boil and boil rapidly until jelly will set when tested.

Blackberry and Rowan Jelly

Gather the rowans (mountain-ash berries) when fully ripe. Pick, wash, and put into preserving pan with barely enough water to cover. Boil for half an hour, stirring occasionally until the fruit bursts. Strain, but do not squeeze. Gather blackberries which are not too ripe (a deep red is best). Place in pan with a cup of water to each 4 cups of blackberries. Boil 20 minutes then strain through a jelly bag. Take equal quantities of blackberry and rowan juice and return to washed preserving pan with 1 cup heated sugar to each cup of juice. Boil 30 minutes, stirring occasionally. Skim, place in glasses, and seal while hot.

Crab Apple and Bramble Jelly

Use 2 parts of blackberries to one of crab apples. Wash and cut up the crab apples. Cook the fruits separately, with just enough water to cover. When tender, strain through a jelly bag. Combine juices and measure. Allow 1 cup sugar to each cup of juice. Bring the juice to a boil, stir in the heated sugar, stir until dissolved. Bring again to a boil and boil rapidly until the jelly will set when tested. Skim and pour into heated jars.

Johnny McGorey Jelly

"Johnny McGoreys" is one name for rose hips, the seed pods of the wild rose. "Sticky-backs" is another name which derives from the fact that children who are full of devilment like to crush the pods and push them down the back of an unsuspecting victim: the prickly fibers can be very irritating.

Ingredients: Take equal parts of Johnny McGoreys, crab apples, blackberries, and damsons. Cut up the crab apples (including peels and cores) combine with blackberries and damsons and add water to cover. Simmer until tender and strain through a jelly bag. Simmer the rose hips separately in cider to cover. Strain through flannel to insure that none of the fibers get into the jelly. Combine juices, measure, and place in preserving pan. Add 1 cup heated sugar for each cup of juice. Boil until the jelly will set when tested.

Loganberry Jelly

Ingredients: 4 quarts loganberries, 2 cups water, 1 cup sugar to each cup of juice.

Method: Simmer the fruit with the water for 30 minutes. Strain through a jelly bag. Measure the juice and return to the preserving pan with the heated sugar. Boil until it jells when tested. Skim, place in glasses, and seal at once.

Parsley Jelly

There are people who swear that parsley jelly can cure every known ill from king's evil to St. Vitus's Dance. Anyway, it is very good as an accompaniment to meat.

Ingredients: 6 cups well-washed, loosely packed parsley, cider to cover, rind and juice of 1 lemon, 3 cloves, 4 cups apple juice, sugar.

Method: Make the apple juice as for apple jelly, *i.e.,* simmer chopped apples in water to cover until pulpy, and strain through a jelly bag. Simmer the parsley in cider to cover 30 minutes. Strain, combine parsley liquor with apple juice. Measure, and to each cup of juice allow 1 cup sugar. Place in preserving pan, add strained lemon juice, and cloves and lemon rind tied in muslin. Add heated sugar. Stir until sugar is dissolved; then boil rapidly until jelly will sheet from spoon. Remove cloves and lemon rind. Place in glasses, and seal at once.

Red Currant Jelly

Fill a crock three-quarters full of crushed red currants and stand it in a very slow oven or in boiling water until the juice is drawn from the fruit. Strain through a jelly bag until the juice ceases to drip. Measure the juice and place it in a preserving pan with 1½ cups heated sugar to each 2 cups of juice. Boil until the jelly will set when tested.

SCENTED JELLIES

Apple or gooseberry jelly is usually used as a base for these special preserves.

Elderflower Jelly

After simmering gooseberry jelly 15 minutes add a good handful of elderflowers tied in muslin to each pint of jelly.

Geranium Jelly

Make apple jelly in the usual way. After jelly has simmered 5 minutes, add 2 sweet geranium leaves tied in muslin to each cup of jelly.

Mint Jelly

Boil a good bunch of lemon mint in 1 cup wine vinegar for 10 minutes. Add to 4 cups apple jelly after 15 minutes' simmering. (Usually served with lamb or mutton.)

Rose Jelly

Tie the petals of 6 cabbage roses in muslin and add to 4 cups of apple jelly after 12 minutes' simmering. Remove rose petals before filling glasses and sealing.

JAMS

Apple Jam

Pare, core, and slice the apples. To each pound of sliced apples allow 1¾ cups sugar, 6 cloves, 4 tablespoons sliced candied lemon peel, and ½ cup water. Put apples and water in preserving pan. Add the cloves tied in muslin. Bring to a boil and simmer gently until apples are tender. Take from fire, remove cloves, and put the cooked apples through a sieve. Return the pulp to the clean pan, add the candied peel, and bring to a boil.

Add the hot sugar, stir until sugar dissolves, then bring to a boil and boil fast until a little of the jam will set when tested on a cold plate. Pour into hot jars and seal at once.

Apple and Rowanberry Jam

Ingredients: 3 pounds sliced apples, 3 quarts ripe rowanberries, 5½ pounds (11 cups) sugar.

Method: Pick the berries from the stalks and wash them. Place them in preserving pan with water to cover. Boil 10 minutes, strain, and add the juice (there should be about 5 cups) to the apples and sugar. Boil until the jam will set when a little is tested on a cold saucer.

Blackberry and Apple Jam

Use ⅓ apples to ⅔ blackberries. Pare, core, and quarter the apples and boil in just a little water until soft. Put through a sieve. Combine the apple pulp and blackberries and weigh. Add heated sugar to equal weight (or cup for cup) of combined fruits. Place in preserving pan. Bring slowly to a boil, stirring constantly until sugar is melted, then boil rapidly until jam will set when tested—about 25 minutes. Skim, fill jars, and seal at once.

Black Currant Jam

Ingredients: 4 quarts black currants, 5 cups water, 6 pounds (12 cups) sugar.

Method: Boil the topped and tailed fruit with the water for 20 minutes. Add the heated sugar, stir until the sugar is dissolved. Bring to a boil and boil rapidly for 5 minutes.

Cherry Jam

Ingredients: 1 pint gooseberries, ½ cup water, 4 quarts cherries, 8 cups sugar.

Method: Boil until pulpy the topped and tailed gooseberries with water. Strain and add the liquid to stoned cherries. Heat until the juice begins to flow, then add heated sugar. Stir until the sugar has dissolved, bring rapidly to a boil, and boil until the jam will set when tested. (This jam should be fairly runny.) One of my happiest memories of Spain is a special treat of

Salamanca: plain cookies spread with creamy cheese of the region and topped with cherry jam.

Damson Butter

Ingredients: 6 cups sugar, 4 pounds damsons.

Method: Cook fruit until tender in barely enough water to cover. Rub through a fine sieve. Combine sugar and pulp and boil rapidly, stirring constantly, until preserve "sheets" when tested.

Gooseberry Jam

Ingredients: 2 quarts (8 cups) prepared fruit, 6 cups sugar, 4 cups water, strained juice of one medium lemon.

Method: Simmer fruit and water gently for about 20 minutes, or until fruit is very tender. If the fruit is inclined to cook dry, a little more water may be added. Stir in heated sugar and lemon juice. When sugar has dissolved, boil quickly until jam will set when tested. (Test for setting point when jam has been boiling about 10 minutes.) Fill jars and seal immediately.

> N.B.: A handful of elderflowers tied in muslin and added about 10 minutes before jam is cooked gives a lovely muscatel flavor.

Lemon Curd

In the top of a double boiler place 1 cup sugar, ½ cup butter, and rind and juice of 2 medium lemons. Add six well-beaten eggs. Cook, stirring constantly, until the curd is thick and creamy (about 25 minutes). Fill jars and seal like jam.

Pear and Apple Jam

Ingredients: 2 pounds sliced pears, 2 pounds sliced apples, 2 lemons, 1½ cups cider, small stick (or 1 teaspoon ground) cinnamon, 10 cups sugar.

Method: Simmer the cinnamon in the liquid for 20 minutes. Strain off the cider through fine muslin and place in preserving pan with sugar. Stir over low heat until sugar is dissolved. Add finely grated lemon rind and strained juice. Add fruit and bring to a boil. Continue boiling until jam will set when tested.

Plum Butter

Wash plums and cook until tender in enough water to keep from burning. Rub through a sieve, measure, and allow 1½ cups sugar to each 2 cups of pulp. Combine sugar and pulp, stir over gentle heat until sugar dissolves, then boil rapidly, stirring constantly, until the butter "sheets" when dropped from side of spoon. Fill jars and seal like jam.

Plum Jam (Whole Fruit)

Wash, halve, and stone the plums. Place the fruit in layers in a crock or bowl, adding 1 cup sugar to each cup of plums. Crack some of the stones and remove the kernels. Tie the kernels in muslin, allowing 4 or 5 to each pound of plums. Leave the fruit overnight. Next day, add the kernels, bring slowly to a boil and boil rapidly until setting point is reached. Do not skim until the jam is cooked. Remove kernels. Leave in the preserving pan until a skin begins to form on the surface, then stir this skin down gently into the jam—this is to prevent the fruit from rising to the surface. Fill jars and seal while hot. A couple of tablespoons of brandy is a nice addition.

There is no preserve which quite equals the delight of the first few pots of summer jam—particularly when the strawberries or loganberries or raspberries or currants have been gathered in one's own garden. I feel that to cook strawberries or raspberries until the jam will set stiffly is to rob the fruit of much of its flavor—and to reduce considerably the final quantity of jam. Far better ensure that the jam will have all the flavor of the fresh fruit by cooking it for the minimum time. What matter if it is slightly runny? What matter if short cooking time usually means short keeping time? In any case, family and friends will see to it that the jam will not remain on the pantry shelf longer than a week or so.

Raspberry Jam (Whole Fruit)

To each pound (3 cups) of ripe raspberries allow ½ cup red currant juice prepared as follows: remove stalks from red currants, place in preserving pan, crush, and simmer until juice runs freely. Strain. Place the currants in preserving pan together with 1 cup heated sugar to each cup raspberries. Bring to a boil, boil 3 minutes; add raspberries and boil 5 minutes longer.

Rhubarb and Gooseberry Jam

Ingredients: 4 pounds rhubarb (12 cups diced), 8 pounds (16 cups) sugar, 3 quarts (12 cups) gooseberries.

Method: Wash rhubarb and cut in small pieces. Place in a large bowl and mix well with sugar. Allow to stand for 24 hours. Drain juice from rhubarb, put in preserving pan, and bring to a boil. Add the rhubarb and topped and tailed gooseberries. Bring to a boil and boil quickly until the jam will set when a little is tested on a cold saucer.

Spring Matrimony Jam

Take 12 bananas, 6 sweet oranges, and 4 lemons, using only pulp and juice of oranges and lemons. Peel the bananas and cut in small pieces. Put all in preserving pan with 1½ cups heated sugar to each 2 cups of fruit. Stir until sugar melts, then boil rapidly 20 minutes. Jar and cover while hot.

Strawberry Jam

Ingredients: 2 quarts (12 cups) strawberries, 8 cups sugar, juice of 2 medium lemons.

Method: Crush the fruit lightly. Put into the preserving pan with just enough water to keep from burning. Heat slowly until the juice begins to flow. Add the sugar which has been heated in the oven. Stir until dissolved, then bring to a boil and boil rapidly for not more than 5 minutes. To prevent the berries from floating the top of the jam when placed in jars, allow the cooked jam to stand for a few minutes in the preserving pan. A skin will form. Stir this down through the jam to anchor the fruit. Fill jars and seal at once.

Tomato Jam

Ingredients: 3 pounds (12 medium) green tomatoes, 6 cups sugar, ½ cup water (about), juice of 1 large lemon.

Method: Skin and chop tomatoes. Simmer until tender in enough water to keep from burning. Add heated sugar and lemon juice. Stir until sugar has dissolved. Bring to a rolling boil and cook, stirring constantly, 20 minutes, or until jam will set when tested. Fill jars and seal at once.

N.B.: Gorgeous with cold meat of any kind.

MARMALADES

Apple and Lemon Marmalade

Ingredients: 6 medium cooking apples, 2 pounds (about 10) lemons, 5 cups water, sugar.

Method: Pare apples and cut them small. Cook in a small amount of water until tender. Halve the lemons, squeeze the juice, and chop the rinds coarsely. Soak the rinds overnight in the water. Next day, bring them to a boil and simmer until tender. Add the apples and the lemon juice and measure. To each cup of pulp, allow ¾ cup heated sugar. Bring to a boil. Boil rapidly until the marmalade will set.

Bitter and Sweet Marmalade

Slice 7 Seville and 12 sweet oranges and 6 lemons as fine as possible, removing pips. Place in an earthen jars and add 3 quarts water. Let stand 48 hours. Place in a preserving pan and simmer until peel is tender. Then add 20 cups (10 pounds) heated sugar and stir until sugar has dissolved. Bring to a boil and cook rapidly until peel is quite soft and marmalade will set when tested.

Blackberry and Apple Marmalade

Take equal quantities of apples and blackberries. Cut up the apples without paring or caring them. Combine the fruit, and add sufficient cider and water (half and half) to keep the fruit from burning. Simmer 1 hour, then rub all the soft pulp through a fine sieve. Measure the pulp, and return to clean preserving pan with 1 cup of heated sugar to each cup of pulp. Bring slowly to a boil, and simmer until it will sheet when dropped from side of spoon. This preserve must be stirred constantly, as it is apt to burn. Fill glasses and seal while hot. The use of glasses will permit it to be turned out whole. It slices like cheese and is delicious with blancmange or cream desserts (or for school lunches).

Carrot Marmalade

Ingredients: 6 medium carrots, 2 pounds (7 medium) Seville oranges, sugar, water.

Method: Scrape carrots and cut them small. Cook in a small amount of water until tender. Halve the oranges, squeeze the juice, and chop the rinds coarsely. Put the rinds to soak overnight in 5 cups water. Next day, bring them to a boil and simmer until tender. Add the carrots and orange juice and measure. To each cup of pulp allow ¾ cup heated sugar. Bring to a boil and boil rapidly until the marmalade will set.

Tomato, Apple, and Ginger Marmalade

Ingredients: 3 medium tomatoes, 1 lemon, 3 medium apples, 4 tablespoons chopped candied ginger, sugar.

Method: Pour boiling water over tomatoes. Leave for 5 minutes. Drain the tomatoes, skin them and chop small. Cut up lemon finely and leave to soak 12 hours in 2 cups of water. Pare, core, and chop apples. Combine the fruit, measure, and add ¾ cup sugar to each cup fruit. Bring slowly to a boil, and boil rapidly until the marmalade reaches setting stage. After 25 minutes of cooking, add 4 tablespoons chopped preserved or candied ginger.

CHUTNEYS

Apple and Tomato Chutney

Ingredients: 8 medium green tomatoes, 6 medium cooking apples, 6 small onions, 1 clove garlic, 2½ cups dates, 1 cup packed brown sugar, 2 cups raisins, 2 teaspoons salt, a generous pinch of cayenne, 4 cups white vinegar.

Method: Cover tomatoes with boiling water. Leave them for a few minutes, then pour off the water and remove the skins. Slice the tomatoes and put them in a stewpan. Add cooking apples, pared, cored, and sliced; sliced onions, and clove of garlic. Add dates (stoned), brown sugar, raisins, salt, cayenne, and vinegar. Boil the chutney until thick and soft, then fill jars and seal like jam. This chutney is excellent with cheese.

Gooseberry Chutney

Ingredients: 5 pints (9 cups) gooseberries, 1 cup sugar, 2 medium onions, 1½ cups raisins, 2 tablespoons salt, 1 tablespoon mustard seed, 2 cups vinegar, a little water.

Method: Chop the onions. Cook in barely enough water to keep them from burning. Add sugar, mustard seed, and vinegar, the chopped gooseberries (topped and tailed), and other ingredients, and cook gently until the chutney is the consistency of jam. Place in sterilized jars and seal at once.

N.B.: An enameled saucepan is best for making chutney.

Tomato Chutney

Ingredients: 2½ pounds (4 quarts or 12 cups) finely chopped green tomatoes, 1 cup vinegar, 2 pounds (12 cups) chopped apples, 2 tablespoons cinnamon, 4 cups raisins (chopped), 2 tablespoons salt, 1 cup finely chopped beef suet, 1 teaspoon ground cloves, 1 teaspoon allspice, 4 cups (2 pounds) brown sugar, ½ cup molasses.

Method: drain the chopped tomatoes and put them in a large preserving pan. Barely cover with boiling water, boil 5 minutes, then drain and repeat. Drain and add remaining ingredients. Mix well, bring to a boil, and simmer until dark brown and thick. Put in sterilized jars and seal. Use as a relish with cold meat, or use as filling for tarts. To use in pie, sprinkle the tomato chutney with raisins, dot with butter, cover with top crust, and bake in a hot (425°) oven about 30 minutes.

Tomato Relish

Ingredients: 7 pounds (about 24 medium) ripe tomatoes, 2 cups vinegar, 8 cups (4 pounds) sugar, 1 tablespoon salt, 2 tablespoons whole cloves (or 2 teaspoons ground cloves).

Method: Skin and chop tomatoes, place with sugar and salt in preserving pan, add cloves tied in a piece of muslin. Cook until as thick as jam. Let stand overnight. Reheat to boiling, remove cloves; fill jars and seal.

PICKLES

Avoid using a methol bowl when preparing pickles. Use instead a china or earthenware bowl. Pickles taste better when the vinegar is spiced. To prepare spiced vinegar, put the vinegar into bowl; add cinnamon, cloves, ginger, and peppercorns in the proportion of 2 teaspoons of each to 1 quart of vinegar if the spices are whole. If ground spices are used, allow ½ teaspoon to each quart of vinegar. Cover the bowl with a plate, stand in a pan of hot water, and heat until the vinegar is just boiling. Leave on one side for about 2 hours. Strain through muslin before using. Root vegetables and mushrooms are cooked before pickling. Other vegetables are pickled raw. They should be soaked in brine before being put into the spiced vinegar. Prepare the brine by bringing to a boil 2 cups salt with 1 gallon of water. Strain and cool before using. Vegetables which are cut up, such as cucumbers and cauliflower, are soaked in brine overnight. Whole onions are soaked in brine for two days. Walnuts should be soaked for a week. Pickles may be stored in sterilized jars or bottles. For sealing, use a large clean cork with a piece of wax paper underneath. A good alternative seal is a piece of wax paper covered with a piece of clean dry cotton which, in turn, is covered with a layer of melted paraffin. All pickles, with the exception of beets and cabbage, should keep indefinitely.

Pickled Beets

Wash carefully, taking care not to break the skin. Boil in salted water or bake until tender. When cold, peel and slice or cube. Pack into jars and cover with cold plain or spiced vinegar.

Spiced Pickled Cabbage

Use red cabbage. Discard outside leaves. Shred the heart finely, put in a bowl, cover with brine, and leave overnight. Next day, drain well, mix with cold spiced vinegar, pack into jars adding vinegar to cover the shreds completely. This pickle is ready to eat in one week and should not be kept more than two months.

Pickled Gooseberries

Dissolve 4 cups sugar in 2 cups spiced vinegar. Bring to a boil and add 3 quarts (12 cups) topped and tailed gooseberries. Simmer gently until fruit is tender, but not pulpy. Drain, and put into warmed jars. Reheat the vinegar until syrupy, pour over the fruit, and cover while hot.

11

Irish Hospitality

"...and when you go forth, you shall not depart empty..."
Exodus III, 21

I never prepare a light snack but I think of Nan Clery and the way she looked after Mrs. Brennan.

Nan was a big, raw-boned girl of twenty when she first went into service at the Brennans'. She had a cheerful red face, and there was a great air of kindness and dependability about her. Poor Mrs. Brennan was badly in need of someone with such qualities. She had found little enough of them in Jim Brennan. From the day they married he gambled and drank everything they owned. Shortly before Nan went to work there, he had managed to get himself drowned in the canal, leaving his thirty-year-old wife with four children and not a penny to rear them.

There was no widows' pension in those days. Rose Brennan went back to the dressmaking. With Nan to look after the house and mind the children for her, she managed well enough.

The years went by and Nan stayed with Rose Brennan, standing beside her in every joy and sorrow that came with the growing up of Paddy and the three girls. She helped to lay out Tessie, the youngest, when she died of meningitis. She packed Lena's trunk for her when she went off to be a nun. She knitted six pairs of socks for Paddy to take to Africa when he got his job in the gold fields. And she helped to dress Clare the morning she married the Dublin insurance man.

The two women had been together for thirty years when arthritis and failing health forced Rose Brennan to put away her scissors and needle and thread. What Paddy earned in Africa was barely enough for the needs of himself and his young wife, and Clare could not spare enough from her husband's salary to keep two homes going.

"You'll have to give up the house and come and live with us," she wrote to her mother. It was a heartbreak on Mrs. Brennan to go. Everything else apart, she hated having to accept bed and board from Clare's husband, who was mean and begrudging. It was an even bigger heartbreak on Nan to put her friend on the Dublin bus, and then start the new job she had found for herself with Old Dinny Twomey of the hotel.

She was miserable there, and we were all delighted when her brother John wrote from New York asking her to come out to him. She had not heard from John for twenty years. Now he wrote to say he had four saloons and that he wanted to make up to her for his long neglect. To prove that he was in earnest, he sent her five hundred dollars to cover her fare and her clothes.

Nan went around for a week with a thoughtful face. Then we saw Dan Dooley hard at work on the little empty shop beside the chapel. When the new sign went up, it said, "Brennan and Clery." And before a month was out, the two friends were doing a good trade in fancy goods and sweets and cigarettes.

Not that Mrs. Brennan was able to do much, for by now she was almost completely an invalid. But Nan had the strength of two women and the willingness of ten, and she was able to spare time from the running of the business to give Rose more care than she would have got in a stylish nursing home.

"This is a mouthful for the Mistress," she would say, taking a little fish custard from the oven—a couple of rolled filets baked in a cream sauce enriched with an egg. "That's the thing to remember about people with delicate stomachs: offer them more than a mouthful and you'll put them off."

You would need to have an extra delicate stomach to refuse Nan's meals. They were served with the daintiness which an invalid appreciates. She never spared those little extra touches which add so much to the look of a dish—a fan of cut lemon with the scrap of fish, a little nut of butter creamed with chopped parsley and chives on a grilled chop, a grating of nutmeg on an egg flip, a ruby of jelly or jam to take the bareness from a glass of baked custard.

The most remarkable thing about Nan Clery was that though she supported and mothered Mrs. Brennan until the day she died, she always referred to the old woman as "the Mistress."

A still more remarkable thing about Nan was her genius for making sandwiches. She was automatically elected commander-in-chief whenever a Ladies' Refreshment Committee was recruited to provide eats at dance, sports meeting, or card drive. I myself served under her the year we ran a series of socials to pay off the food debts of twelve-child widow McCaffrey the year old Ned Grogan was threatening to put her in jail.

Like people the world over, our usual offering to chance callers was sandwiches, cakes, and a drink. And our usual sandwich recipe had been, "Put a slice of bread or cheese between two slices of bread." But Nan Clery widened our horizon. Nan's repertoire of fillings equaled a course at the Cordon Bleu. "There's luck in sharing" was Nan's motto—as indeed it is of all Irish people who are worth their salt.

In those twelfth-century *Triads of Ireland* which I mentioned early on, there is a golden rule for hostesses. It goes: "Three uncomfortable welcomes: a house busy with handicrafts, scalding water over your feet, salty food and no drink to follow." This is why, when a friend brightens our threshold, all work ceases and the best in the house is put on the table. To make sure that we are never caught without plenty of sandwich fillings and canapé spreads, we like to keep a variety of potted savories in the pantry. And let this be said in our defense when our many faults are being totted up: our hospitality embraces even that trying type of guest of whom it is said, "If he went to a wedding, he'd stay for the christening."

Potted Ham

Ingredients: 2 pounds lean ham, ½ pound pork or ham fat, ½ teaspoon ground mace, ½ teaspoon ground nutmeg, ½ teaspoon pepper, ¼ teaspoon cayenne, clarified butter (melted and strained through muslin).

Method: Put the ham and fat through a fine food chopper and pound thoroughly in a mortar with the seasoning. Put in a buttered bowl, tie down with buttered paper or foil, and steam 2½ hours. When cooked, pack into small sterilized pots, cover with clarified butter and tie down with foil or wax paper.

Potted Liver

Ingredients: ½ pound streaky bacon, 1 pound pork liver, 1 pound pork sausage meat, 1 teaspoon salt, ½ teaspoon pepper, ½ teaspoon allspice, 2 bay leaves.

Method: Slice the bacon thinly, remove rinds, and cut up. Cut up pork liver and put with bacon through a fine food chopper. Combine with sausage meat. Mix evenly with spices and seasonings and place in a buttered bowl. Lay the bay leaves on top. Tie down securely and steam 3 hours. Remove bay leaves. Pack into small sterilized pots, cover with clarified butter, and tie down with foil or wax paper.

Potted Dublin Bay Prawns

Ingredients: 1 quart prawns, ½ cup butter, ¼ teaspoon cayenne, ½ teaspoon grated nutmeg, 1 teaspoon salt, clarified butter.

Method: Boil shell, and devein prawns. Chop roughly, then pound to a paste with butter and seasonings. Rub through a sieve, press into small pots, cover with clarified butter.

N.B.: All potted meats or fish should be tied down with paper or foil when cold.

SOFT DRINKS

Apple-Ade

Bake 6 large apples without paring them. When cooked, place in a large jar, pouring over them 6 cups boiling water; add 7 cloves and 1 teaspoon grated lemon rind. When cool, strain through muslin and sweeten to taste with honey. Drink undiluted.

Carrageen Lemonade

Ingredients: ¼ cup carrageen moss, 1½ cups cold water, lemon juice and sugar to taste.

Method: Soak moss in cold water for 10 minutes. Place in top of double boiler and cook in the water 30 minutes. Strain and add lemon juice and sugar to taste. Drink when cold.

Elderflower Lemonade

Ingredients: 1 pint lightly packed elderflowers, 1 gallon water, 1 lemon, 3 cups sugar, 2 tablespoons white wine vinegar.

Method: Put all ingredients in an earthernware crock (lemon should be cut in quarters). Leave for 24 hours, stirring occasionally and giving the lemon a slight squeeze. Strain and bottle, tying in corks securely. Lay the bottles on their sides.

Harvest Drink

This is the drink with which generations of haymakers have slaked their thirst. Pour a little tepid water on ¾ cup ground oatmeal. Mix well, then add ½ cup sugar and 2 lemons, thinly sliced. Add 1 gallon boiling water, stir well, and leave until cold. Gently pour the clear liquid off the sediment and serve very cold.

Raisin Tea

Boil 3 cups chopped raisins with 5 cups water and ¼ cup sugar. Boil rapidly uncovered until reduced to 4 cups. Strain and add the juice of 1 lemon.

Rhubarb Drink

Cut up 1 dozen large stalks of rhubarb and boil until tender with 4 cups of water. Strain and place in a large jug. Melt ½ cup sugar in a little boiling water and added to the rhubarb juice together with the juice of 2 lemons.

Of all drinks offered in an Irish household, the most usual and most popular is tea. But there's none of your "teabag" nonsense about Irish tea. We make sure that the kettle is boiling, and the teapot is scalded. We use one spoon of tea for each person and an additional spoon "for the pot." An important point: the water must be actually boiling when it is poured on the tea, so we take the pot to the kettle—never the kettle to the pot. And we let it "draw" near the heat or under a tea cosy for a good 5 minutes before we pour it.

I have no statistics of the actual consumption of tea per capita in Ireland, but I'd be willing to wager that it is higher than in China. I myself drink tea at least six times each day. In fact, my love of tea once inspired me to write:

When everything is rosy and I want to jubilate,
    Do I run around rejoicing over town?
No; I set the kettle boiling and I sit and celebrate
    With my little shiny teapot, colored brown.

And when the skies are gloomy, do I languish in despair,
    Although Dame Fortune turns on me her frown?
I walk into my kitchen, for there's comfort waiting there
    In my little shiny teapot, colored brown.

Friends may come and friends may go, and love they say is rare.
    I know a friend who'll never let me down.
And when St. Peter calls me, this will be my earnest prayer:
    "May I bring my shiny teapot, colored brown?"

SLÁINTE
(Good Health)

Beet Wine

Ingredients: 5 pounds beets, 20 cups (5 quarts) water, rind of 2 oranges and 1 lemon, 1 cup barley, 9 cups sugar.

Method: Cut up the beets and boil in the water until tender. Strain. Add the orange and lemon rind, barley and sugar. Boil 10 minutes. Strain. Bottle and cover. Set in a warm place to ferment. Warning: If you cork the bottles tightly before fermentation has ceased, you are likely to find your kitchen strewn with broken glass and flooded with wine.

Blackberry and Apple Wine

Ingredients: (1) 9 quarts (36 cups) blackberries, 12 quarts water, 2 cups barley, 24 cups (12 pounds) sugar. (2) 4 pounds apples, 4 quarts water, 2 cups rice, 8 cups (4 pounds) sugar.

Method: Simmer the blackberries and 12 quarts of the water for 15 minutes. Add the barley and boil 10 minutes. Strain. Add the sugar and stir well. Cut up the apples without paring and boil 15 minutes in 4 quarts of water. Strain, add the rice, bring to a boil and boil 5 minutes. Strain. Add the sugar and stir well. Combine the two liquids. Put into bottles and cover. Do not cork until the wine has ceased to ferment, *i.e.,* until small bubbles cease to come up and break on the surface. It is this "working" which refines the wine. Inspect the bottles daily or almost daily during the 2-3 months' period needed for fermentation. If the wine is not "working" the temperature is too low, and the bottles must be moved to a warmer place. For good fermentation wine must be kept in a room where there is constant heat.

For a clear, sparkling wine, thorough straining is necessary. Strain first through muslin, then through two tea-towels, and finally through a glass funnel in which you have placed a ball of cotton wool.

Blackberry Mead

Ingredients: 2 cups barley, 5 quarts water, 1 teaspoon grated nutmeg,

4½ quarts (18 cups) blackberries, 1 pound (3 cups) plums, 8 cups (2 quarts) honey.

Method: Boil the barley in the water 15 minutes. Add the nutmeg, blackberries, and plums. Boil 10 minutes and strain. Add the honey. Stir well, strain, bottle, and cover.

> N.B.: This is one of our modern versions of the mead which, in days gone by, was known as "the dainty drink of nobles." There was a time when County Meath men were very stuck-up because one historian referred to them as "the mead-drinking men of Meath."

Black Currant Liqueur

Ingredients: 2 cups rice, 4 quarts water, 3 pounds (6 cups) black currant jam, 4 cups (1 quart) honey.

Method: Boil the rice in the water for 3 minutes, then strain. Add the black currant jam and boil for 6 minutes. Add the honey. Stir well and strain. Bottle and cover and leave to ferment in a warm place.

Black Velvet

This is a half-and-half mixture of champagne and what we Irish call "the wine of the country," *i.e.,* Guinness stout. While this is a good drink, I am a believer in the saying that of two good things you shouldn't make one inferior thing. Which is why I prefer my champagne or my stout neat.

Gaelic Coffee

Into a 6- or 8-ounce stemmed glass pour one jigger of Irish whiskey. Fill glass to within half-inch of brim with coffee—hot, black, and strong. Add sugar to taste and stir well. Float about 3 tablespoons of lightly whipped cream on top. The coffee should not be stirred after cream is added: the charm of this drink (apart from its enlivening effect) is the contrast of hot and cold as one drinks the hot whiskey-laced coffee through the cold cream.

"Will you? was never a good fellow" is an old saying, which is why, whether we are helping our guests to whiskey, stout, wine, or tea, we never put the superfluous question: "Will you have another?" Instead, we pour the drink with the comment, "A bird never flew on one wing" or "It wasn't on one foot that St. Patrick came to Ireland."

And if the host should forget his manners and serve himself first, he will be excused if he says, "The priest always baptizes his own child first." This is not a reflection on the celibacy of our clergy but a reference to a never-to-be-forgotten Kilkenny event when a woman presented her husband with seven sons at the one birth.

The distracted man saw no future for himself or his family, so he rushed out of the house with the intention of drowning himself in the Nore. On the way he met the local parish priest to whom he confided his suicidal intentions. "Take it easy, man," the priest advised him. "I'll rear one of the children. And we'll find neighbors who'll be glad to take some of the others off your hands." And so it happened. At the mass baptism, the child adopted by the kindly parish priest was the first to be baptized. They say that the seven brothers are buried at Freamstown, County Kilkenny.

Our toasts are many. "Sláinte" (Good health) is the most common. "Sláinte 'gus saoghal agat" (Health and long life to you) is equally popular. A more elaborate toast goes:

> Health and long life to you
> The woman of your choice to you:
> Children without end to you,
> Land without rent to you,
>   And death in Ireland.

My own favorite is the toast which takes care of the future: "May you be seven years buried before the devil knows you're dead."

The Haunted Girl

Mother, don't chide me for the way
I never hear you when you call,
Nor for the idle way I stare
Into the turf-fire all the day.
My head is ringing with an air
That troubles me since I was small.

Mother, when I was very small,
You tied a bonnet on my head
And sat me in the grass one day,
And made for me a cowslip ball.
Be good, said you, sit there and play
While I go in to bake the bread.

And, Mother, while you baked the bread
And I played near the hawthorn bush,
A burst of singing broke and fell
In golden rain about my head.
'Twas then he bound me in his spell,
That speckle-breasted fairy thrush.

Oh, Mother, blame that runing thrush
That I don't bake or sew or sweep,
And that I never want to wed.
For once, below a hawthorn bush,
A thrush's singing filled my head
And lulled me into fairy sleep.

Index